SURVIVE — an

Inc. magazine surveyed 400 small business books for its cover article: "In Search of the Small Business Bible." After selecting the top 40, they seriously investigated those 40 to determine which offered, in their words, the best advice delivered with authenticity and a broad vision.

When Friday Isn't Payday won "Best of Show." Here is what they said:

"My favorite section of *When Friday Isn't Payday* is called, 'Dealing with Crisis.'...This is Kirk at his best, an experienced small business owner figuratively at your side, keeping panic at bay with practical solutions.

What separates this book from the pack is its relentless practicality... the book wins high marks for knowing the territory -- and covering it well."

Launch and Grow Rich is the first half of When Friday Isn't Payday. I wanted to offer this complete guide to the start up phase as a stand-alone book. If you prefer, you can buy the entire book on Amazon at bit.ly/WFIP_3

Here's a bulletin from Randy W. Kirk, founder of twenty different small businesses including AC International which boasted of over $5 million in annual sales: "Only half of all start-up businesses will be around to celebrate their third birthday! What's the secret of success for a small business? It's attitude!

- Do you expect success?
- Are you prepared for failure?
- Can you conquer your fears?
- Will you do the hard things?

If your answers are yes, you're ready. **Launch and Grow Rich** is the Real Life Course 101 of small business advice guides."

Bonus Content—Free Access for Life

200 Pages is a large enough book. And *Launch and Grow Rich* is designed to be an introduction to almost every aspect of planning and starting a small business. Some of the sections just beg for a deeper dive. Throughout the book, you will find the following URL mentioned: https://WhenFridayIsntPayday.com When you choose to get the rest of the story, you will find hundreds of pages of additional content. Here are some of the titles:

The Elon Musk Method

Elon Musk is a true entrepreneur. He has more ideas than he can possibly manage at any given time. So, he chooses a vision, creates a plan and executes. This article will reveal the special approaches that Musk uses, and that you can emulate.

Doing the Hard Things

Most owners of the small business are their own worst enemy. And most of the time this is due to one huge roadblock. They are unwilling to do the hard things. We'll delve into the list of hard things that seem to be thwarting small business owners and offer ways to get past them.

40 (at least) Fundamentals of Marketing

Commonly, the decision to go into business for oneself does not include any education, experience, or knowledge of marketing. Like any skill set, marketing has a set of fundamentals. Explore the 40 most basic fundamentals.

More Bonus Content

Funding Your Small Business the 21st Century Way

Not so very long ago there was a local banker who knew you well enough to loan a new company a decent sum on signature alone. Not true today. However, there are still plenty of ways (like equity crowd funding) to fund a good business. Some of them will surprise you.

Finding Hidden Diamonds in Financial Statements

What is the purpose of a Profit and Loss Statement? Balance Sheet? The best way to think of these tools would be health measurement tools for your business. Used correctly, they will commonly be the biggest money maker you have at your disposal.

Masterminds – What Was Napoleon Hill Thinking?

In 1924 Napoleon Hill wrote a book called Think and Grow Rich. In this book, he described many common elements of highly successful business people. He stated that these individuals all had mastermind – a group of people whose combined knowledge, experience, wisdom, and inspiration were critical to the owner's success. Learn how to find a mastermind group or start your own.

Fundamentals of Networking

In the age of smartphones, it might seem as if meeting prospects, clients, and networking with other owners and professionals might be so analog. Quite the contrary. Networking groups, mixers, and events designed to provide human contact are all the rage. Learn how to become a skilled networker.

Even More Bonus Content

Online Marketing – from Websites to Facebook and More

It makes no sense at all to put online marketing advice and directions in a permanent format like a book. It would be outdated before the ink was dry. The solution! We will keep this online material updated and fresh for you at all times.

Kickstarter to Amazon

Up until about 10 years ago, the investment necessary to bring a new product to market was daunting. Now you can test a new idea on Kickstarter $5000 or less and hone the product and the message in preparation for selling the item on Amazon. Here's how.

How to Reach the Goals You Set

Goals, resolutions, plans, and dreams. Every owner has these in abundance. Why do so many go unrealized? There are methods and techniques you can use that will dramatically improve your execution of the goals you set. We offer the best approaches.

Comparing Corporate Structures: S vs LLC vs C

When it comes time to incorporate, don't choose an LLC because it sounds cool. There are huge differences in taxation and other ramifications to this choice.

Managing Your Time

How much time do your employees spend on Facebook when they are on the clock? Better question. How much time do you waste on Facebook and other rabbit trails? Here's help.

Launch & Grow Rich

Start Up Your

Small Business

Money Maker

RANDY W. KIRK

This publication is designed to provide competent and reliable information regarding the subject matter covered. However, it is sold with the understanding that the author and publisher are not engaged in rendering legal, financial, or other professional advice. Laws and practices often vary from state to state and if legal or other expert assistance is required, the services of a professional should be sought. The author and publisher specifically disclaim any liability that is incurred from the use or application of the contents of this book.

Copyright© 1993, 2006, 2019 by Randy W. Kirk All rights reserved.

Send Me Press

Library of Congress Cataloging-in-Publication Data Kirk, Randy W.
Launch & Grow Rich: Start Up Your Small Business Money Maker/
Randy W. Kirk, p. cm.

1 6 3 1 0 9 5 0 2
Library of Congress Control Number
Launch & Grow Rich: Start Up Your Small Business Money Maker

9 7 8 1 7 9 2 6 0 8 3 6 0
ISBN

1. Small business—Management.
2. New business enterprises—Management.

Cover design by: Sah Mabalay

This book is dedicated to Toni Kirk

I am not at all certain that this book would exist but for the encouragement of my best friend and sweet wife.

Press on: Nothing in the world can take the place of persistence. Talent will not; nothing is more common than unsuccessful individuals with talent. Genius will not; unrewarded genius is almost a proverb. Education will not; the world is full of educated derelicts. Persistence and determination alone are omnipotent.
—CALVIN COOLIDGE

...accomplish in one year more than you could accomplish without it (a mastermind group) in a lifetime
- Napoleon Hill -

Join an Online MasterMind Group and Experience Personal and Professional Growth Beyond Your Greatest Expectations

If you are a business owner or you are independent in your position AND you have a strong desire to become more successful, the MasterMind is the solution you've been looking for.

- ✓ Peer-to-peer direction and consultation
- ✓ Peer group accountability
- ✓ Like having your own personal board of directors
- ✓ Meet with others who understand you
- ✓ Get clarity about your objectives, goals, hopes, dreams, and expectations

Learn More at https://OnlineMasterMinds.Biz or email RandyKirk77@Gmail.com

Contents

Introduction

No knowledgeable person denies it; the facts are undeniable. Even the federal government recognizes the reality. The very small businesses of America are the economic engine of the twenty-first century.

The Fortune 500 only employs 17% of the population today, and the mom-and-pop establishments across the country have more than made up for this deficit. There are millions of businesses throughout our nation and the world that have fewer than ten employees on their payroll. Most of these companies were smaller than that in the past, and never will be much bigger. Here is the first amazing fact: **Most have no desire to be any bigger.** And amazing fact number two: **Most of them would not be better off as a result of being larger.** In fact, many of these owners would make less money . . . with more headaches.

If you're reading this book, you're either already in business or are seriously considering taking the plunge. Many in your shoes have the mistaken belief that bigger is better. Many have visions of multistoried office buildings with hundreds of employees scurrying this way and that, all at their bosses' beck and call.

There's absolutely nothing wrong with wanting to own and run a large organization. This book, however, is founded on the premise that there's also nothing wrong with a business whose staff never includes more than ten employees. It's possible to earn well into six figures, or even seven, with a staff of nine. You can sell a small business of this type for millions of dollars.

As an entrepreneur who has founded and operated twenty-one such companies, I can attest that there is virtually no literature that tells an owner/manager how to open such a business, or how to run it. Almost every business book written has in mind an operation made up of hundreds, if not thousands, of employees. A few magazines try to reach this group with at least part of their editorial content. Unfortunately, articles providing basic information and help for the very small business are infrequent and hard to find.

So where does that leave the new business that plans to start and stay small? You may be able to find a mentor in a local service organization or church congregation. Valuable help is available through the chamber of commerce and networking clubs such as TEAM and others. Unfortunately, none of these resources is really going to provide you with the depth of information you need to plan, start, develop, and—when the time comes—divest your business.

I thought about doing this book for almost five years before I started writing in earnest. During that period I wrote two books for the specific industry in which I make my living. Both of these books and the numerous articles I published in trade magazines dealt with one of the most quaint examples of under-ten- employee ownership, the bike shop.

Then one of the businesses I was involved in broke past the ten- employee level and grew to over one hundred. During this growth, I realized that I'd never expected the business to become that large. I'd often pointed out that I preferred the environment of a very small enterprise. It was at this point that I really felt the call to get this book into print.

Launch and Grow Rich is divided into the two clear-cut stages of the small business launch.

In section 1—Before You Begin—we take a look at what it really means to be an independent businessperson. What is a myth and what is a reality in terms of finances, hours, and sacrifices to home and hearth?

The purpose of section 1 is to provide you with information that will help you make a choice about going into business or not. Section 1 also provides an overview of the types of enterprises that are available and the personality types that offer the best fit.

Section 2—Opening the Doors—picks up after the decision is made to go into business. Presented first is "the plan": a simple, step-by-step procedure for developing a fundamental business plan.

Next, the section looks at some legal considerations. To incorporate or not to incorporate . . . licenses, permits, leases, and insurance. By the time you're through with this section, you'll wish you were an attorney.

Selecting service vendors such as a bank, CPA, lawyer, or insurance agent can be a real can of worms. How do you decide which one to use? How do you work with these folks to get the most out of these relationships?

A major cause of new business failure is inadequate record keeping. Section 2 will explain the fundamental principles of accounting and offer recommendations about how to approach bookkeeping's most challenging hurdles.

For many businesses, the selection of a location can be the most important decision the new owner makes. "How large, how much, and how's the traffic?" are but a few of the elements that go into this important process. Detailed strategies are provided, including how to negotiate with the landlord.

Next, we consider the specifics. What kind of business is it? How do you find out if you have a large enough population to support your new enterprise? What vendors are available to supply you? Have the best suppliers already given exclusives in your preferred neighborhood? How do you establish credit with the sources you'll need to provide your opening inventory, fixtures, supplies, and services?

You've had the grand opening, and everything is perfect. Well, almost everything. There are not nearly enough customers to pay the bills. One of your suppliers was out of product when you called to replenish what you sold at the opening sale. Plus, it's become all too clear that you don't have enough capital to keep going if the business doesn't pick up soon.

It's my sincere hope that the approaches discussed in the following pages will help you create a solid business asset—one that can be redeemed for a high return on your investment, should you ever decide to retire.

Once again, I want to stress that hundreds of additional pages are available online to supplement the materials here. Please watch for the links throughout the book. **https://WhenFridayIsntPayday.com**
These additional pages are designed to provide you with more depth that could be included here. As you can well imagine, the potential amount of material you could consume dedicated to opening a small business could fill a bookshelf or two. This book has been carefully pared down to provide you with the basics that should be sufficient to start you on the right track.

Think of Launch and Grow Rich as the foundation and some of the structure. The online materials will provide you with more of the structure where you feel you need more help. And sometimes you will fill the need to go beyond the online material to other books, tutorials, or even classes to really dig deep and become expert.

And then I'll leave you with this thought about being an expert. You undoubtedly have some skills, training, or certifications that make you an expert in the business you plan to start. Maybe you have a law degree or you're a trained beautician, or you have ten years of experience in auto repairs and some certifications. It is obvious to you that you wouldn't pursue the type of business you are contemplating without your expertise.

The reality is that it should be just as obvious that one

shouldn't contemplate opening a business without expertise in the subjects covered in these next pages. You need to be an expert at counting. You can't manage what you can't count. Thus we have standard accounting methods for helping you keep count.

You need to be an expert in sales or sales management. Somebody is going to need to sell for the company.

You need to be an expert in marketing or be prepared to pay for outside help to make your company visible, to lay out your store if you are in retail, and to manage your online presence.

While it may seem daunting that you need to be an expert in so many areas, don't allow that to even slow you down. It doesn't take much to become well versed in the areas you need to for business. Dig in and do the hard work. It will pay you huge dividends in the future.

SECTION ONE

Before You Begin

CHAPTER

1

Why Self-Employment?

So, **you want to own your own business**. You're not alone.
The idea of being in business for oneself is as American as apple
pie or baseball. It's the rare American who hasn't at least
considered the idea from time to time. (This is not to say that
the goal is unknown in other nations or cultures. In fact,
citizens of Australia and Taiwan have an even higher level of
interest in self-employment than do citizens in the United
States.)

Many do take the plunge. From selling Avon or Amway to
purchasing a McDonald's franchise, from marketing a brand-
new idea to hanging out a dentist's shingle, from buying out
their boss to opening a hardware store, millions of otherwise
intelligent folks give up good-paying jobs and sink their life
savings into being their own boss.

What would motivate a person to risk his livelihood, his marriage, and his emotional health? Why would a person want to
work sixty or eighty hours per week for little or no income? Who
are these entrepreneurs who give up the safe life for a taste of
life in the fast lane? What is the big deal, anyway?

Money? The pursuit of the almighty dollar and all that goes
with it? Are we a nation of aspiring Elon Musks? Yes, and no.
Many, if not most, of those who choose the path of self-
employment

expect to make more money than they could as an employee. They're willing to put up with inconvenience and temporary poverty in order to create a high-income position for themselves in the future. Those primarily driven by monetary considerations also generally expect to "get rich." But the lure of excellent pay alone is not appealing enough for most folks to agree to even temporary sacrifices. If it were, we'd see these individuals taking a safer route to the same end, such as furthering their education, job hopping, or going into commissioned sales jobs . . . not starting a business.

Personal independence takes a close second to hard cash in driving an employee to become a boss. This type of individual may find it hard to work for others, or simply want to do it *his/her* way. Folks who find being employed by others about as desirable as swimming with sharks don't care how successful they are in business. They'll keep the doors open regardless of the sacrifice to self or family. They'd rather be operating a one-man shoe-repair store than be vice president of a $10 million division of a conglomerate. You'd be amazed at how many small retailers fit into this category. You'd be even more surprised to learn how many doctors, lawyers, CPAs, and other professionals make substantially less than their potential income in order to be "on their own."

Among those entering the world of self-employment is the managerial-level woman who has what it takes to run a business, but who has hit the "glass ceiling." That is, while her employer may talk a good game about equal opportunity, and may have made great strides in this area, there's a point above which there is still a sign on the door: **no women need to apply**. Thus the talented and motivated female often finds that the only hope for reaching her full potential is to open her own enterprise.

Another large group of small business owners is motivated by a desire to make a special contribution to the world—one they believe would be impossible to make working for a profit-seeking enterprise. Here you'll find the hobbyist who wants to make sure other model-train collectors in Dubuque have a place to buy, sell, and trade their collections.

Also in this group are the lawyers who wish to provide low-cost legal services to special segments of the population who couldn't otherwise afford a lawyer; doctors, dentists, and other professionals with similar motivation; pastors of independent congregations; founders of specialized schools, cooperatives, and credit unions. The list of those who find small business an outlet for their community-service orientation goes on and on.

Interestingly, this selfless approach often results in much greater financial success than the business founded to create wealth, probably as a result of the tireless devotion that such an enterprise produces. When the primary goal of an owner is making money, it's common to see great swings in the level of desire. When the going gets very rough or too easy, many who have only dollar signs in their eyes lose interest. Those who are pursuing the greater good may feel a stronger compulsion to keep on pushing.

Simply being out of a job has often pushed people into self-employment. This seems to be particularly true when an individual has lost his job due to a merger, an acquisition, a dot-com bust, or changing economic conditions (the rise of China as a competitor).

Having something to prove can be a major motivational factor. A parent, sibling, spouse, or another significant person who is doing well in his own business, or speaks of others who are, could create pressure to give it a try. A rival is making more money than our budding businessman. He sees a small venture as the only hope he has of "keeping up." A son feels that he must keep the family business going, or do it *better* than his dad. This group may be acting from a neurotic point of view, and as such will likely be very unhappy in business. Some of our most successful and well-known businesspeople are very wealthy and very unhappy because their drive comes from this unhealthy direction.

Only rarely does an individual who aspires to a life of self employment fit just one of these categories. More frequently, there is a mixture of forces at work. For instance, the desire for financial independence coupled with a need to call all the shots is a potent combination. The overriding fact remains that, for whatever reason, many in our population will take a stab at going it alone. There's something very romantic—and very American— about owning your own business.

In this section, we'll try to take a slightly less passionate look at ownership. Our goal will be to provide a set of practical guides that will allow you to come to a logical conclusion about whether you should go out on your own. Every attempt will be made to give you an overview of every aspect of the decision-making process.

CHAPTER

2

Do You Have the Right Stuff?

Being your own boss will likely be the hardest thing you'll ever do in life. This is not meant to scare you, intimidate you, or even discourage you from trying. It's simply a fact.

Being the boss means making important decisions every day from less-than-complete information and experience—decisions that could destroy the business you've built and all that goes with it. You alone can make these decisions, regardless of the input, you might get from employees, partners, spouses, or outside professionals. When all is said and done, it's up to you, and you'll harvest the fruits of your decisions . . . sweet or bitter. This is why we say, "It's lonely at the top."

If you have a friend or relative who owns her own business, she's probably bored you stiff with complaints about the hours she must work, her cash problems, or the loss of a major customer. There's a tendency to see her problems as overstated. Because you have a working acquaintance with hiring, firing, pricing, collections, and lawsuits in your current employment, you believe that you have an insight into how tough it really is. *You don't.*

If you run out of cash at home, you borrow twenty or fifty dollars from a co-worker until Monday. If the crisis looms larger, you might tap your brother or dad for a thousand bucks until your tax refund comes in. When you run out of cash in a business, where do you go to make a fifteen-thousand-dollar payroll tomorrow morning? How do you come up with thirty thousand dollars to repay the bank today when failure to do so could mean the bank gets your business *and* your home?

When your favorite grocery store goes out of business, you drive a few extra blocks and shop somewhere else. When a supplier of one-of-a-kind merchandise closes, where do you find a new source to make up the 30 percent of your sales that that vendor's merchandise represented? What expenses or which personnel do you cut if you can't find a way to make up the lost sales?

When you make a decision to rent or buy your home, you sign a long-term document that means you have an obligation to pay some amount each month to stay there. If you try to get out of a rental agreement on an apartment, it might cost you a few months' rents. If you try to abandon a mortgage, it will rarely cost you more than your original down payment. When you rent a piece of commercial property, however, you may be signing a document that puts you on the hook for hundreds of thousands of dollars whether you succeed in your business or not.

As an employee, you may have complained about the extra work on your desk when your assistant quit and moved out of state. You faced this extra burden at least until you could find and train a replacement. Imagine the headaches you'd have if your right-hand person in a three-man shop left to open his own place down the street... in competition with your fledgling enterprise.

Now you're sure this is meant to scare you off. Not at all. It's meant to suggest that just as the weak-kneed shouldn't try hang gliding, the weak-minded shouldn't go to medical school, and the weak-spirited should forget small business.

If you have the right stuff, nothing is more fun, more challenging, or more rewarding than being at the controls. There are times when your heart will be in your throat, and times when you'll feel as if you're carrying more than your shoulders can bear. However, there are few experiences in life as exciting as landing the biggest account in your field or scratching out your first profitable year. There's real exhilaration in knowing that you're creating careers that are supporting families. It feels good to build something, even if it's just a hundred-thousand-dollar-a-yeartax-preparation outlet with yourself and one employee.

The very first set of questions you should ask yourself is: "Am I willing to put up with sixty-to-eighty-hour weeks the first four or five years? Do I want to be on an emotional roller coaster for the rest of my career? Do I have the stomach for making several tough decisions every day that might affect not only my own investment but the livelihood of employees and their families? Is my family ready to cut back financially if necessary?" Then there's a big one: "Am I mentally prepared for failure?"

Now is a really good time to stop. Go back. Reread the last paragraph and think about each question. Unless you can be honest with yourself regarding these questions, your continued reading of this book will be largely wasted. You may protest that you really won't know the answers until you've tried it, and no one could argue against you on that point. However, it's essential that you give the best answer you can because it is a lead-pipe certainty that you'll find yourself in each one of those circumstances.

Let's take another look at that last one. *Failure!* You *will* fail. Even if your enterprise is a success (and you've certainly already seen the statistics on that), you'll endure many failures on the way to success. Even if you were to follow every idea and approach in this book to the letter, the varieties of circumstances facing a new enterprise are infinite. ***Business is a process of succeeding from one failure to the next.***

Thus, a real measure of the potential of any individual who wants to make it in business boils down to how that person handles failure Examine yourself in your present endeavors. Do you pick yourself right up after an expensive mistake and keep on keeping on? If the customer says no to your sales pitch, do you still pick up the phone and call the next prospect?

When you work for someone else, you may be able to go into a slump for a few days after a major let down. If you're on commission, it may affect your income that month. However, unless your sales manager is extra tough, you probably won't see any lasting consequence of being "off" for a few days.

When you own the store, you have no such luxury. If anything, you have to be ready to work harder and smarter after a failure than before. Think hard about this. Don't let your ego get in the way of an honest evaluation. *Do you have the mental and emotional toughness to get back up on the horse immediately after you've been thrown and put the spurs in deep?*

Next, let's consider the issue of work habits: Don't believe for a minute that you're going to be successful working forty-hour weeks. For the first few years, expect to spend almost every waking hour either working at a specific task related to your enterprise or at least thinking about it.

We're not just talking here about whether you have the stamina to put in long hours. The issue is whether you have the willingness to put everything and everybody else on hold until you have the ship afloat. Your spouse and children will be the ones most directly affected, but it will also take a toll on your friends, other relatives, sporting interests, hobbies, and, of course, your TV habits. When you first start out, you'll even have to give up vacations. Not until your company is big enough for you to turn things over to a trusted second-in-command will you be able to afford the luxury of more than a long weekend.

Doubtless, some of you are skeptical. "C'mon," you're saying. "I agree with your premise that I'm not trying to be the next Microsoft. I just want a nice little business that nets me a cool hundred grand a year. Surely I can do that in forty or fifty hours per week and not bring my problems home to the bedroom."

No. No. And no. It just doesn't work that way. Whether you're starting a future General Motors or an ice cream parlor, the first several years are going to require your undivided attention if you have any hope of success. An associate of mine didn't buy my advice; he set up a retail business with the full intention of working nine to six with an hour lunch, five days a week. The company is still in operation today, although my friend now has a 75 percent partner. Worse than that, the business generated no take-home income for five years. One can only guess at the success that might have been attained with 25 percent more effort.

The next question would seem to be an obvious one, but so often this is the very issue that sinks the budding entrepreneur who otherwise has everything going for him. Are you a self-starter? An early riser? A go-getter? Three different questions? No, all three are the same.

Most people need management. They need someone to jump-start their motor when they have an off day, week, or year. They need a mentor to fill in the blanks of their knowledge and experience. They need a patient listener to bounce ideas off of or to complain too. They need a team to help with the brainstorming when the idea well runs dry.

The newly self-employed can kiss all those luxuries good-bye. Your spouse may or may not want to fill some of those roles. Ironically, the spouses who are the most capable of providing help in these areas are usually married to folks who might accept that advice and help from anyone *but* their husband or wife.

Parents, friends, and old business associates might be able to help with ideas during a crisis. There are many kinds of associations you can join, such as mastermind groups that will broaden your knowledge and provide networks of businesspeople similarly situated. The fact remains, however, that you're going to have to do 90 percent of the hard stuff on your own.

There will be mornings when you're certain that someone has

put Super Glue in your bed. You'll try to convince yourself that it really doesn't matter whether you open the doors at 9:00 a.m. as dictated by the posted hours. No one is ever there that early anyway.

Try to picture yourself in a retail setting. You arrived at 8:30 a.m. It's now three in the afternoon and the door has yet to open except for the hourly trip you make to the sidewalk to see if the town is still populated. You've restocked the shelves. You've posted all the receipts. You've even taken out the broom and cleaned up the place. You know in your heart of hearts that you should now pick up the phone and find some excuse to call a few customers and offer them a good reason to come in. You consider in your mind a few ideas you've read in trade magazines for improving traffic flow. Unfortunately, selling over the phone and planning promotions are not your favorite thing to do. You have no real experience at either one, and you're nervous about trying your hand at them.

If you can see yourself in the picture above, think long and hard about going out on your own. You're going to have to do *whatever it takes* within the bounds of legality to make your business go when it ain't. If you prefer to be closed on Sunday, but you're not paying the rent, you have to be open on Sunday. If you're in a service business, you'd better join a few organizations like the Rotary, the Chamber of Commerce, or TEAM Referral Network even if you're not the joining type. You will gain important information just from joining, but you'll have to be active if you're going to make contacts.

No matter what line you decide to pursue, you're going to have to *sell*. Many, if not most, new businesspeople don't like to sell, have no special gift for selling, and have absolutely no training in selling. Those of you who fit the above description are now arguing out loud with the idea that you must sell your product or service. You're absolutely convinced that your idea is so amazing, and that your future customers are so needful of your stuff, that they'll beat a path to your door based on internet exposure alone.

You couldn't be more wrong! Nobody ever has—or will in the future—beat the door down to buy any legal substance. If ever there was a product that amazing, the competition would spring up within days to cut short this perfect opportunity.

There are many ideas in this book that will help you immensely if you follow the broad precepts. On the other hand, there are a few "golden nuggets" that are so important; they really do represent the difference between a big success and a bigger failure. Here's the first golden nugget. *Learn to sell.*

Selling is a profession. In its finest form, it is at least as difficult as doctoring, lawyering, or pastoring. There is no profession that requires more continuing education. The truly great salespeople are constantly learning new approaches and reviewing the old standards.

You needn't be suave, charming, or brilliant to be a good sales rep any more than those traits benefit a CPA or an engineer. What you need is a good grounding in the specific skills that make for sales success. There are hundreds of books on the subject. Read them. Reread them. Keep them handy. Be prepared to read them again during the first few months after opening, because *Nothing happens until something is sold.*

Let's review what we've covered thus far. Being your own boss is hard. You'll work harder than you ever have before. You'll need to work smarter than you did as an employee. You'll be the president in charge of everything—including *selling.* You'll be all alone at the very moment when you need a big, experienced team. You'll very likely have to reduce your standard of living, and you may forget what some of your family and friends look like. The question is not "Do I want to attempt this life?" Rather, the question you should ask yourself (with the hope that you'll give yourself a very honest answer) is "Can I do it? Do I have the mental and emotional tools necessary to handle running a very small business?"

Go deeper with online articles explaining the benefits of mastermind and networking groups. Look for page 19 at https://WhenFridayIsntPayday.com

CHAPTER

3

What Will It Cost?

The world is just full of wonderful ironies, and the world of small business is no exception. For instance, the primary motive for going into business is financial independence, a state of affairs in which a person, by definition, "no longer has to concern himself about money on a day-to-day basis." So what a twist it is that the good soul who chooses the path of self-employment will spend the next several years thinking about little else besides money.

Unless you're one of the very fortunate few who've already reached the state of financial independence, the lack of money will very likely provide you with your biggest hurdles in the first years of business. Initially, you have to find enough cash to open the doors. A huge percentage of entrepreneurs start their business knowing they're undercapitalized. The rest find out soon afterward.

Later, if you've been able to generate enough cash to keep the place open during the early stages, you'll need to find ways to raise capital for expansion.

Finally, just when you think you have it all figured out, the economy, your business, or both will go into a slump and you'll need a cash fix to bail yourself out.

I've started very small businesses with as little as five thousand in cash and as much as fifty thousand dollars. Neither was nearly enough. I've seen friends start service-oriented enterprises out of their homes that you might think would need very little cash. Within weeks of opening, they found they'd gone through twenty or thirty thousand dollars.

Every book or brochure on start-ups stresses the importance of sufficient capital for both the business and your personal overhead. Most suggest that you have enough funds to pay your personal expenses for six months to two years. *No one ever does.*

In days gone by it was possible, although difficult, for the owner of a small enterprise to get by without knowing too much about financial statements, cash-flow analysis, tax planning, and other tools of the money-planning part of running a business. Hard to believe, but there was even a day when a person could run a fairly big operation without a computer. Even just twenty years ago, I knew quite a few owners who were trying to get by without financial and computer skills. They were at a huge disadvantage. In this highly competitive time, you can't afford to give your crosstown rival an inch.

If you have any thought of taking a run at this game, you must get some serious training in accounting, business finance, and computers *now*. There are several good books available, and every junior college and university offers beginning courses in each of these subjects. You'll also get a cursory look at these subjects in later sections of this book. The more you know about money, the better chance you will have of managing it.

So what will it really cost to get started? The flip answer is "All the money you (and any of your friends or relatives foolish enough to lend it to you) have." The thoughtful and realistic answer is "You're probably going to open the doors with whatever you have anyway, so get as much as you can." Section 2 will get into more specifics, but let's take a look at some general ideas of the starting expenses you're likely to incur. You'll need to determine the legal form your business will take.

The expenses of opening will vary depending on the form you choose.

■   Sole Proprietorship. This approach is the least expensive, but riskiest, way to start out. (We'll discuss other aspects of these legal ideas later. For now, a sole proprietor is a form of business where you are the only owner, and you have not incorporated.) You can probably handle all the legal expenses of starting a sole proprietorship for under two hundred dollars.

■   Partnership. A partnership (which is like a sole proprietorship except that there are two or more partners) will cost substantially more. Most partnerships are simple arrangements where you and a friend or two go into business together. That is where it stops being simple. You need to decide how each partner will contribute to the enterprise in money and time, and how each will benefit in salary, ownership, and other compensation. Decisions need to be made as to who will do what, when, and how. It is also a good idea to know what will happen if one or more of the partners want out. These and other subjects are usually covered in a partnership agreement. Although it is possible to start a partnership without this agreement—and no law requires one—it is, however, a very good idea to prepare such a document to help settle possible disputes later on. A lawyer will charge you anywhere from two thousand dollars and up to prepare this little document. There are books in the library and information online that you could use to help you prepare your own. If you take this route, you would still want an attorney to look it over.

■   Limited Partnerships. This is a business form where there's one partner or group of partners called general partners who are generally active in the company. Another group called limited partners are merely investors. This form has some characteristics of a partnership and some of a corporation. The legal costs associated with beginning a limited partnership would range from five to fifty thousand dollars. This form of business is associated with enterprises that are more sophisticated than most first-timers are going to try.

■ Corporations. The best approach for most new firms is going to be incorporation. It is not very expensive, and there are many benefits. Depending on whether or not you use a lawyer, and varying somewhat based on the complexity, you can handle the legal expenses of a new corporation for one to five thousand dollars. (If you're planning to offer stock to the public the cost will be closer to fifty thousand.) There are three types of corporations, Sub "S," LLC, and "C." There is no significant difference in set up cost between these three types.

As for licenses, fees, and taxes, this category of start-up expense will vary greatly depending upon the type of business you intend to enter. There are ways to reduce these specific expenses. Section 2 provides you with thirty years of experience at *legally* beating the system.

At a minimum, you can probably expect to pay one hundred dollars in unavoidable levies to the various governments that will have their hand out. If you're planning to open a professional office or a highly regulated operation like a restaurant, your total outlay in this category could run easily into the thousands, or even tens of thousands, of dollars.

Office supplies and basic equipment will cost at least two thousand dollars. You'll need to print letterhead and business cards. Most new companies will need to purchase a computer, an all-in-one printer, and miscellaneous office supplies, as well as establish an e-mail address and create a basic website. You may also need to leave deposits with the utilities and set up online accounts with UPS and FedEx.

Fixtures could hit you the hardest of all. Manufacturers need production equipment, installation of electrical and plumbing systems, shelving, tools, and shipping supplies. Wholesalers will find it hard to operate without shelving, a UPS scale, shipping tables, and quality dollies. Retailers can easily spend five to ten thousand or more on display cases, wall displays, specialty equipment such as clothing racks or jewelry cases, and mood-setting items such as carpet, paint, and lighting.

Service industries may have even greater outlays in the fixture department. Dentists, doctors, and veterinarians have huge outlays for the tools of their trade. Beyond that, there may be even more expenses for waiting-room furniture, patient record supplies, and uniforms. These same kinds of outlays await lawyers, CPAs, interior decorators, and others who are service providers.

Next on the list is facilities. Many small businesses are operated out of the home, but for most types of enterprise, this just isn't practical. This is an extremely important area. Many young companies that go under in the first year do so because they can't make the rent.

If you need to rent a space for your firm, you'll have to figure an initial outlay of at least first and last months' rent plus any leasehold improvements (changes made to the building for your type of business). Since you're just beginning, it's likely that your landlord will be looking for three months' rent to move in. All the issues raised here are subject to negotiation, and section 2 offers plenty of ideas on how to reduce your rent and your up-front payout to the landlord. For this aspect of your open-the-doors cost you'll want to figure anywhere from one thousand dollars for a seven-hundred- square-foot warehouse space in a rural area with no leasehold improvements to twenty thousand dollars for nine hundred square feet in a major urban retail setting with minor build-outs. (Please don't confuse this range with the different issue of monthly rents. This is what it will cost you to move in.)

Yes, it *is* starting to add up. Unfortunately, we haven't come to the really big ones yet—inventory and receivables. Some businesses keep no inventory, and there are a few companies that can get all of their customers to pay cash on the barrelhead. For the rest (almost all) of us, these two items usually represent the biggest numbers on the balance sheet.

Example: An extremely well-run retailer may be able to "turn" his inventory four times per year. This means that the store will sell four times its average inventory (in dollars, at cost) each year. To briefly explain, let's work through an example. If a store stocks an average of five hundred dollars in product and sells that product at a 50 percent margin (buys the product for $1 and sells it for $2), and is able to turn it four times, it will have $5,000 at 50 percent margin ($10,000) times four turns, equaling $40,000 in sales.

Since there are very few retailers who could make it on $40,000 in sales their first year, let's use $100,000 as the first-year sales goal instead. Second, a 50 percent average margin is a good goal for most general retailers (with many exceptions), but that mark-up is also unlikely the first year due to probable discounting to attract customers. Let's use a 40 percent margin instead. Finally, an inexperienced retailer is not going to turn his product four times. Let's be conservative and use three turns. One hundred thousand dollars in sales after three turns equals $33,333 after a 40 percent mark-up, which means $20,000 in average inventory.

Our retailer in the example may be able to get some help from his suppliers in allowing credit terms for payment. Unfortunately, unless you have a great personal balance sheet, most suppliers are not going to offer trade credit to a start-up. They'll want to ship to you at least once or twice on a COD basis before offering you a small credit line.

Manufacturers and wholesalers have the double capital burden of carrying inventory *and* "carrying" their customers' receivables. Today, the companies who carry receivables can expect to get paid forty-five to sixty days after shipment (exceptions in both directions abound). Thus, if you hope to do $300,000 in sales your first year (a modest goal for most wholesalers and manufacturers), you can expect to carry $300,000 divided by 12 months in a year ($25,000) multiplied *by 1.5* months (average time from sale to payment), resulting in $37,500 in receivables. The money that you "loan" to your customers is *cash* you won't have available to spend on new inventory, payroll, or the rent.

There are many other potential items to consider in arriving at the starting capital necessary to open the doors. Some are: an advertising budget for a grand opening and ongoing marketing; outdoor signs; a down payment on vehicles; an accountant's fees and software for setting up a bookkeeping system; special bonds for certain industries; computers.

Finally, there's the question of staying power. How many months of operating expenses are you going to put aside as a hedge against missed sales expectations? You're going to have to pay fixed overhead expenses such as rent, payroll, payroll taxes, and utilities even if no customers succumb to your terrific sales pitch.

Depending on the type of business, you should probably have about three to six months' worth of hard expenses set aside, including enough money to cover your personal expenses for the same period. For a single individual starting a service business out of his apartment, this may be only a few thousand dollars. For a married manufacturer with children to feed and a payroll to meet the amount could total tens of thousands of dollars.

4

Basic Budgeting

What does all of this add up to? The best way to find out is to construct a budget. If you decide to go forward with a career as a business owner, you'll be constructing lots of budgets. Happily, this is the least difficult of all financial documents. It is really little different from the kind of budget you use at home.

Of course, it's possible that many reading this don't have a household budget, and wouldn't know how to create one. What follows is a very simple budget for starting a small retail establishment.

I'll use a fictional bike dealer as our example. Most of what will be covered would pertain to all types of small enterprises. For many of you, some of these amounts may seem small, but they're representative of the time and the place in the example.

Jimmy wants to open his new shop in a suburb of Dallas. He's worked for an established bike store for a couple of years (very good idea) and feels he's ready to go out on his own. He has savings of $35,000, and he has an excellent credit rating. He's single, but dating, and shares an apartment with a roommate.

Jimmy was making $2,850 a month as a manager for Smith and Sons Petaluma. After taxes and $300 per month for his savings account, he has been spending about $2,200 on personal expenses.

Jimmy decides it would be a very good idea to see just how little he can get by with for the first year after he opens. He starts with a personal budget.

Item	Amount
Rent	$ 790
Food	220
Car Payment	200
Gas/Repairs	120
Car Insurance	120
Telephone	75
Gas	30
Electric	70
Water	15
Clothes	40
Entertainment	50
Charity	10
Gifts	35
Household	100
Medical/Dental	150
Payments	25
Misc.	50
Total	$2,100

After taking a look at his checkbook and tax file, and charting his cash expenses for a month, the above budget emerges. Jimmy is able to cut $100 a month from his spending. However, he's unable to see how he can save anything beyond that without giving up his car or moving back in with his folks. He decides to use this amount as a basis for his first six months in business to see if his savings will hold out.

Next, he constructs a projected budget for opening the doors.

Item	To Open
Legal	$ 350
Office Supplies	100
Office Equipment	150
Store Fixtures	2,500
Shop Tools	700
Rent	3,000
Build-Outs	2,500
Inventory	20,000
Advertising	3000
Accounting	450
License/Fees	150
Telephone	300
Utilities	1000
Signage	1000
Total	$35,200

Right away Jimmy can see he has a problem. His opening expenses are going to be $200 higher than his total savings. He won't have a cent left to pay expenses for the first month of operation, or any income for himself. This is exactly the kind of information that you'd expect good budgeting to provide. With these findings in hand, Jimmy can now become a manager. He can make decisions. His first decision is to go ahead and look at the operating budget for the first six months, anyway (see page 30).

It's evident from this budget that the conservative way to open this business is with capital (real, hard money, cash dollars) of $60,000. It's rare that anyone is that conservative, however. In fact, a more common approach to the above would be to open the doors with the $35,000 available and borrow the balance. Typically, entrepreneurs such as Jimmy would try to open even if they had only $10,000 cash. The balance would come from credit extended by suppliers, friends, relatives, and MasterCard.

Item	To Open	Month 1	Month 2	Month 3	M
Legal	350				
Office Supplies	100	25	25	25	
Office Equipment	150				
Store Fixtures	2500				
Shop Tools	700	50	50	50	
Rent	3000	1500	1500	1500	
Build Outs	2500				
Inventory	20000				
Advertising	3000	150	150	150	
Accounting	450	100	100	100	
Taxes					
License/Fees	150			100	
Dues/Publications					
Payroll/Payroll tax				1000	
Interest					
Postage			30		
Telephone	300	100			
Utilities	1000	150	150	150	
Shows/Travel					
Signage	1000	1500			
Owner Draw		2100	2100	2100	
TOTAL	**35200**	**5675**	**4105**	**5175**	

Opening with such a bare minimum of invested cash and a great dependence on borrowed funds is defined as leverage.

There's only one problem with leverage. When you're trying to move a ten-thousand-pound boulder with a ten-foot lever your success is based less on your skill at boulder moving than it is on your weight. To make certain this concept is fully absorbed: The ten-thousand-pound boulder is the prospect of your success, the lever is the credit extension that must be paid back and usually comes with interest (expense), and your weight is your own investment.

The real point of this exercise, though, is to give you a formula that will enable you to determine just how much cash you'll need to open your doors. Going through this process is a fundamental step you must take in the decision-making process.

There are substantial online materials that will take you deeper regarding this subject.

Look for *Doing the hard things* where we examine this reality. Businesses often fail because owners won't do the hard thing. Above, the hard thing would be waiting another year and saving more money.

Also, find more examples of start-up budgets.

Go to **https://WhenFridayIsntPayday.com** and look for page 31

5

What Kind of Business?

A major benefit of being in business for yourself is the ability to choose a job that suits you perfectly. True ☐ False ☐

Clearly, the above statement is true. We all have the ability to make that selection. Unfortunately, few ever do.

The most common reasons a first-timer has for selecting a given business are:

1. He works in that industry now.
2. He's worked in that industry in the past.
3. A relative has offered her a chance to take over a going concern.
4. An associate has talked him into selling Amway or Mary Kay.
5. She goes to an opportunity fair and a salesperson talks her into parting with thousands of dollars to start her own print shop, car wash, or hamburger stand.
6. He's an active or past hobbyist in that field.
7. He's always dreamed of owning that type of establishment.
8. Someone she knows is doing well in a similar business in another town.
9. An idea hits him.
10. She can buy an existing business for a bargain.

The preceding list certainly doesn't cover every possible situation, but each reason stated has one thing in common: by themselves, they're lousy reasons for going into any business.

The next few pages will help you with an intelligent approach for deciding which way to jump. It could help you avoid years of wasted time and huge amounts of wasted greenbacks.

WHAT DO YOU LIKE TO DO?

It may be that the idea that an individual should enjoy her work was something dreamed up by the baby boomers while they were going through college. In any case, it has been so reported. Horrible as it is to imagine, there is evidence that past generations may not have concerned themselves very much with the question "Will I like it?" in choosing their vocation.

There are two reasons a person would *not* want to earn a living doing something that he or she truly enjoys. One: a belief that turning an avocation into a vocation would destroy the enjoyment of the first. Two: a worry that if the job is too enjoyable it will mean too much time spent working and not enough time spent with spouse and children.

Where there is smoke, there is fire; thus, I would agree that there is potential for either of the above to come true. However, the potential benefits far outweigh the possible pitfalls. Getting and staying motivated is a critical ingredient in any career. It's a whole lot easier to "keep on keeping' on," even when things are really bleak if you really enjoy what you're doing.

The challenge here is to figure out what you enjoy doing. It's one thing to recognize that you're good with your hands or really enjoy music. It's quite another thing to consider the other elements that go into making a career based on those interests.

For example, let's take a look at a field crowded with hobbyists turned professionals: computers. You really enjoy poking around on a computer. You're better at it than anybody you know. You have a roomful of equipment, programs, and manuals. You subscribe to a stack of industry publications, and you belong to two computer clubs.

It's likely you can succeed in a business related to computers. The question is... which one? Are you really interested in what makes the machine tick and probing the depths of programs? In that case, you might do well as an independent consultant helping other businesses implement specialized requirements for their systems.

Maybe you're primarily interested in applications. You may be able to make it as a programmer, inventing ways the computer can help with tasks, and writing software that gets you there.

Another possibility is that you're most intrigued with the latest products being offered for personal or business use. Every new item that comes out makes you drool. You might find success as a retailer of computer products.

Maybe every Saturday morning your house is filled with neighborhood kids wanting to help you play with your computer. The thing is, you're happy to help them. You're as excited as they are by their explorations into the world of electronic information. Could a computer school or camp be in your future?

So far, we've looked at the enjoyment issue on two levels. The job gets a little tougher as we look at level three. If you were to go into that type of business, what would you really spend your time doing? The computer school provides a great example.

What you enjoy is working with computers, and working with kids and computers. A computer school could provide a great outlet for those interests, but running a computer school would entail far more than that. Call the owner of a computer school in a town far enough away that he won't feel reluctant to give a potential competitor ideas and discuss what really goes into the job. It might look something like this.

Activity	Percentage of time used
Teaching Kids	35%
Selling Parents	15%
Hiring and Training	20%
Administration	20%
Planning Curriculum	15%

The first thing you notice is that the total is 105 percent, and that is probably an understatement. The second thing you notice is that you'll spend only about 35 percent of your time working with computers and/or with kids. You may get some additional computer time as part of your administrative duties, but it's hardly the same. You'll get computer and teaching involvement as part of hiring and training teachers, but will you love working with adults in this environment as much as you enjoy helping the kids?

Then there is "selling parents," or how about "administration"? Do you really want to do all these things? You probably won't be able to hire a person to do them in the beginning. Maybe you never will. Is there another business that you could create to give you the good parts without the bad parts?

How about designing tutorial programs that would let kids teach themselves? To do this effectively you'd have to work with kids to make certain your system is working. You'd spend another large part of your time writing programs and tutorials. The rest of the job would require selling your output. If you're not much of a salesperson and don't want to become one, it's possible to find agents to sell for you.

Now you can begin to see that it's possible to design a business around your particular interests in an effort to make your work fun and interesting. Of course, no matter how perfectly you match this enterprise to your personality, there'll still be tasks that you don't particularly like to do. The idea is to keep these to a minimum.

6

Business Types

THE NEXT FEW PAGES WILL LOOK at broad categories of industries and services so as to acquaint you with the wide range of opportunities available to match your needs with a specific business.

Manufacturing/Importing. Did you ever stop to think about it? Everything has to be made by somebody. Some things are obvious, like cars and refrigerators, but someone also manufactures the door handle and the lock on your car. Some other company makes the keys and the little pins and springs inside that lock. Another company fabricates the machine that puts the lock together.

To succeed as a manufacturer you'd want to have some affinity for machinery and knowledge of certain aspects of the raw materials specific to the type of manufacturing in which you have an interest. It would also be important to know how to motivate factory workers. Most manufacturers also understand cost accounting and enjoy finding methods of doing the job better, faster, and cheaper.

Selling the output of a factory takes many forms, but the owner will usually be actively involved in sales activities. The potential client list of this category would include an OEM (original equipment manufacturer). In this type of arrangement, the output of one factory is sold to another for a component part of the second factory's output. In our example above, the springs, pins, and keys would be OEM parts for the ultimate lock manufacturer, and the lock would be an OEM part for the car manufacturer.

Another customer for a factory's production is distributors. The use of a distributor allows the manufacturer to deal with fewer customers than if that factory were to sell directly to the distributor's customer. By taking this approach, the factory owner can concentrate his resources on making product rather than fielding a large sales force and managing a large accounting department.

Some makers would rather sell directly to retailers. Some call this "eliminating the middleman" (the distributor). The customers here could range from the local mom-and-pop retail store to Wal-Mart.

A big market for manufacturers is the government; federal, state, and local. If you decided to sell to this market, you'd want to have an interest in such pursuits as exacting contract writing, meeting rigid specifications, and dealing with bureaucracies and bureaucrats.

Some companies that fit into the category of manufacturers sell directly to the consumer or, as what is sometimes called, the end user. This is true for the maker of anything, from handicrafts sold at a swap meet, through producers of certain computer programs that sell through their own mail-order lists, to producers of specialized equipment, such as robotics or respirators, that sell to factories or hospitals.

Wholesale distribution. Called variously wholesalers, distributors, jobbers, or feeders, these individuals are the middlemen of business. They generally don't manufacture anything, although some may put their own brand or label on products made by others. Their customer is the retailer, large and small. They may also sell to some end users and to government agencies.

The wholesaler must have special skills, such as warehouse management, purchasing, and collections. He will also be fielding a large sales staff made up of poorly paid salespeople. It takes talent to find and motivate sales personnel in any case, but it's particularly difficult when the financial motivation is lacking.

Sometimes the wholesaler's success derives from the specific product lines it carries. This may occur when a wholesaler has an exclusive for sought-after products in a specific territory. In most cases, however, the successful distributor is one who maintains a high level of service combined with a competitive price for products readily available from competitors.

Manufacturers' representatives. In this business, you operate as an independent commissioned sales representative for one or more manufacturers. Many manufacturers don't want to invest in maintaining their own sales staff. This is partly because quality salespeople command large salaries and thus create a big fixed overhead. It also has to do with independent manufacturers' reps having ready access to the customer. A company that fields its own salespeople must spend valuable time and effort to find and develop customers on its own.

There are few small businesses riskier than that of the rep. If he doesn't do a good job for a company he represents, he'll be terminated. Even if he does a great job, there's a chance that the company will decide it can perform the sales function less expensively with its own sales force. In the meantime, the rep must constantly maintain relationships with existing buyers and work hard to build new relationships with an ever-changing buyer lineup. To make matters even more interesting, all this risk is taken on a commission basis (where the rep is only paid based on how much he or she sells). To add insult to injury, it is sometimes difficult to collect commissions due.

To enter this field you need aggressiveness tempered by great charm. You must be a top-flight professional salesperson. If you're to grow beyond a staff of one, you'll need excellent skills in sales management and bookkeeping.

Sales reps fall into the same categories as the manufacturers they serve. They'll sell to original equipment manufacturers (OEMs), distributors, dealers, end users, or government.

Retailers. This is probably the most familiar category to the average person. Almost every store on the boulevard is either a retailer or a service provider. In a general sense, the operation of a retail store is a perfect job for the jack-of-all-trades. The owner of such a shop usually holds down every job at one time or another, including the janitor.

The most important skill that a small, independent retailer can possess is salesmanship, but sadly, it's frequently missing. Other important skills include purchasing, store layout, and design, inventory management, and hiring and training of clerks. The retailer must be prepared to be open seven days a week, fifty-two weeks a year. Finally, the successful retail store owner must be a good promoter. She must be able to create traffic (customers walking into the store) as inexpensively as possible. Ads on the Internet, window banners, sidewalk sales—these are but a few of the countless methods employed to entice the consumer to drop by and check out the merchandise.

Service providers. This group may be the most diverse of all. Restaurants, print service providers, doctors, lawyers, beauty salons, and tax preparers all fall into this category. Their customer may be anyone from the individual consumer to other businesses or the government. A print shop is a good example of a service provider who has a customer base of just about everybody.

Most of the members of this group are trained and licensed in a special skill. In addition, the small shop must have all the abilities mentioned above in the retailer section. On top of all of that, these folks commonly provide their service on credit, so they must also be good at collections. As a rule, they're not.

Retailers and service providers who hope to enjoy their life in business should like interactions with the public. They should have a strong desire and need to be of help to perfect strangers. Individuals who make their customers feel that they're really on their side and desirous of sending them home with exactly what they need will have great success and happiness as a retailer or service provider.

Those who depend on traffic for a living must also expect to deal with days or weeks when there is little or none. If you're the type of person who goes stir-crazy if you don't have a clear-cut task always awaiting, you may wish to avoid retail and service-type enterprises. The best personality for this type of business is the go-getter who can effectively use dead time to come up with ways to create traffic on future days.

The building trades. It might seem logical to call a home builder a manufacturer, an architect, a service provider, and a building-materials supplier a retailer. It would, but it isn't a tidy fit. This is a completely different world. Very few folks just decide one day that they'd like to become a contractor. This industry requires you to come up through the ranks. It is one of the few places where you'll find the guild system still in effect, with future owners doing their apprenticeship out on the construction site.

If ever there was a type of work that needed owners who love their job, this is it. You either fit in at the construction site or you don't. It isn't absolutely necessary that your hands are rough and calloused and that you have a perpetual tan, but it doesn't hurt.

When you're in this business, you don't get the contract because you have the best salesman. Sometimes you don't even win a contract on the strength of your reputation for good work. Most of the building industry uses a bid system, wherein the lowest bid wins. The balance of your success or failure may rest on whether you're a member of the "good ole boys' club."

Multilevel marketing. Here we have the army of individuals who fill the ranks of independent sales workers for such organizations as Amway, Avon, doTERRA, Scentsy, Mary Kay, and Pampered Chef. Most of these businesses are run on a part-time basis and are highly structured activities where the supplier of the merchandise provides a complete set of materials, samples, and training.

To run this type of enterprise you generally don't need a formal organizational form (such as a corporation), a special business location, or fixtures. There's also generally very little, if any, financial outlay for the product. Since the risk is very low, the reward opportunity is fairly low as well. Only a superstar will make more than twenty or twenty-five dollars per hour for her actual sales effort.

The real money in most of these organizations is the establishment of a "downline" (other independent salespeople recruited by you whose sales result in an override or commission to you). This is called multilevel marketing. There is any number of persons who've started a multilevel business on a part-time basis while holding down another job or working as a stay-at-home parent. Some of the most successful have turned investments of under one hundred dollars into millions, with thousands of people working under them in their downline.

There exists a broad range of individuals who can find success in the multilevel marketing world. It offers an opportunity to those who would be pleased to pick up an extra couple of hundred dollars per month by selling products to friends and family. This type of enterprise may also offer the perfect challenge to the hard-driving individual who is not afraid to stop perfect strangers anywhere to convince them that they can get rich selling that product line.

If you're the second type you'd need to be prepared for the following: (1) Recruiting and motivating individuals who're not professionally trained and may not care about earning more than a little spare change; (2) preparing and running sales meetings heavy on enthusiasm and motivation (in other words, you'll do best in this area if you like to lead the singing at church or have an enthusiastic attitude that you can share from the podium); and (3) doing most of your work on evenings and weekends, because that's when your part-timers are most likely to be available to attend meetings and workshops.

In the area of multilevel marketing be careful to ensure that you're joining a legitimate organization. Based on current law as this book is being written, the primary difference between a responsible multilevel marketing group and one that is not is as follows: The responsible organization is in the business of selling product. The illegitimate group is in the business of selling distribution agreements.

You can generally determine which is the case by looking at two aspects of the contract: (1) If the cost of joining the organization is high or requires a very large outlay for samples, supplies, or fixtures, you may want to look more closely at this company. (2) If you're able to buy into a high distribution level, rather than starting as a salesperson and moving up in the organization by recruiting others to sell, you should investigate very carefully before going further.

Franchises. A business form still very popular today is the franchise. A franchise is an exclusive territory purchased by a prospective businessman from a company that has established a successful model business. The company (called the franchisor) proceeds to duplicate that model by using independent owners (the franchisees) rather than owning their own locations.

Franchising is used for a wide variety of business types but is probably best exemplified by fast-food stores, real estate offices, convenience stores, print services, and greeting card outlets.

The benefit of franchising is that you're given a blueprint of exactly how to proceed with the business. A quality franchisor provides help in site location, store layout, and design, planning a grand opening, co-op advertising, management classes, and bookkeeping aid. This gives the franchise a leg up on success since many of the pitfalls have already been discovered in the test locations. The new franchise doesn't have to lose precious time, money, and energy plodding through those same problems. *As a result, the success rate for franchise purchasers is dramatically higher than for start-ups using any other approaches.*

Unless you're dealing with a McDonald's or other well-known franchisors, there *are* a number of potential problems that come with using this approach. Many successful businesses believe that they can easily duplicate themselves across the country by starting a chain of franchises. What they don't realize is that franchising is like any other enterprise. It has its own unique skill and temperament requirements. Just because a person has put together a fantastically successful ice cream store doesn't mean she'll automatically have the ability to establish a successful national chain.

Even with the noblest of intentions, it's all too common for the franchisor to fail to train the management of the new locations properly, not perform as promised on advertising, and even fall short of producing enough product for its member stores. Unfortunately, too, there are more than a few franchisors who've recruited folks to open locations where the entire deal was a fraud from the outset. In other words, you should use the same amount of care in approaching franchising as you would with any major purchase . . . and then some.

Many studies have been done on franchising because there is a great deal of money to be made by everyone concerned. One of the most interesting conclusions to result from these studies concerns the type of person who is likely to be most successful with a franchise. It has been determined that individuals who have backgrounds working in big corporations have the best chance. This is because they're used to working within a framework dictated by some impersonal third party. They're also good at following directions to the letter without questioning.

On the other hand, the person who has worked in a small office or plant, or who had a business of his own in the past, does not do as well. These individuals are too independent. They want to do things *their* way and are offended by having to take orders from those above. This is especially true if the orders don't square with how the franchise owner sees things.

Another major issue with regard to franchising is the cost. First, the cost of purchasing a territory can be very high—

indeed $10,000, $20,000, or even more just for the right to open a store under the franchisor's name. Next, the start-up costs will usually be higher than would be the case for an independent store. This is because the franchisee must follow all the requirements of the contract. A quality franchisor will have set very high standards to ensure a high success rate. Finally, the business must pay an on-going fee to the franchisor. This fee pays for the continuing privilege of using the name, management training, and joint advertising and PR. This monthly amount might be anywhere from 5 percent to 15 percent of sales, depending on the services rendered.

For the person with the right personality, plenty of start-up capital, and a cautious approach to learning about the franchisor, this entrepreneurial experience can be very satisfying, personally and financially.

We cover two more categories online. First, online sales working with companies like Amazon or eBay. This is now a major way to sell products.

Second, we cover importing, taking a look at companies like Alibaba, but also more traditional ways of finding and marketing products made throughout the world and sold in another part of the world.

Find both of these at **https://WhenFridayIsntPayday.com** look for page 44

CHAPTER

7

Buying a Business

Many who decide to give up a steady paycheck for a dream
pursue that dream by purchasing somebody else's used one. It's
possible that they may be buying a nightmare. Even if the
current owners tell you the truth, the whole truth, and nothing
but the truth, you may still find yourself in all kinds of traps
that neither you nor the old owners ever imagined.

Key employees might leave. Important customers may have
been buying from the company because of the personality of the
owner rather than the quality and service. Once you take over,
these customers may decide to shop around. Equipment that
has functioned perfectly for decades may wheeze to a stop the
second day you own it. These are but a few of the problems you
may face even if you do a fair bit of research and your seller is
perfectly honest.

But should you fail to investigate the business from top to
bottom, or should the seller be adept at keeping key
information out of your hands (for example, a major new
competitor is about to begin producing the product), you may be
finished before you start?

Finally, there is a sleeper issue that has recently surfaced in
some new research. The failure rate for newly purchased businesses is almost exactly the same as the failure rate for start-
ups. The reason for this should be obvious. There is very little

difference between the two types of businesses from the stand-point of the new owner's ability to succeed. She either will or will not have the necessary skills; be willing to put in the needed money, time, and effort; and/or be blessed with good luck. These three elements have more to do with whether a new business succeeds than the rightness of the idea or the length of time the idea has been tried.

The kind of person best suited to take over a going concern would be one who likes to buy fixer-upper anything: cars, houses, furniture, whatever. When someone has decided to sell their business, there's a reason. That reason probably has something to do with the current owner's age, health, or interest level. It may also have to do with the prevailing business climate for the company's products or services. The buyer's job is to hit the ground running so that he can hold on to as much as possible of what the former owner did right. Then the owner must quickly evaluate how it may be possible to fix the things that are broken.

It's also critical that the purchaser be a good listener, and be willing to be very open to the advice of the departing owner. Good on-going communication between the old and new owner is one of the most important ingredients for success in a takeover. In this respect, following the lead of the old management is not unlike entering a franchise situation. If the new management wants to travel their own road from the start or fails to use the experience of the old team to help them around the potholes, they'll have to endure the same learning curves experienced when building a company from scratch.

The financial aspects of purchasing an existing enterprise can have great advantages over the start-up. It's often possible to buy out the old owner for less than it would cost to open a new operation. Often you'll be able to get the business for the cost of inventory or less.

In addition, the seller may be willing to "take the back paper." This means that he may be willing to let you pay some or all of the purchase-price over time. He may do this to facilitate the sale or to take advantage of tax breaks.

If you're patient, you can find a real deal. There is no end to the examples of people who've taken over excellent businesses for no money down and little or nothing later. They were able to get such a deal, for instance, just because the retiring owner liked them and felt they would be good to their customers and employees. So spend some time in the search phase of this approach and you could win big.

CHAPTER

8

The Partner Issue

Should you or shouldn't you take a partner? Do you want or need the help in skills, management, or money? Is there enough potential income to make two, three, or more of you independently wealthy? Are you ready to deal with this type of relationship?

The question of partners is probably more personal than any other. Taking on a partner in business is not very different from taking a partner in marriage. In fact, you'll probably spend more hours per week with your office "spouse" than with your marriage partner. You'll certainly communicate more. You're likely to fight more. Plus, if things don't work out, the decision to end a partnership may be more difficult and more emotionally trying than ending a marriage.

With that said, involving a partner can make great sense in business. Everyone needs someone to motivate them and to hear their ideas and honestly evaluate them. Brainstorming is twice as productive when you have two brains, and both have a commitment. How comforting it is to feel there will be someone to pick up the slack if you're sick or just in a slump. These roles can be nicely performed by the right partner. In addition, a good partner can bring needed management skills with him. He may also have contacts, customers, or product lines that he can deliver to the new company. Clearly, the partner adds productivity. Each partner should be able to produce as much as you do.

In general, there are some economies of scale. The rent, phone, and electricity will not double for two partners over what they would be for each one if they were operating independently. Two (or even three) partners may be able to share an administrative assistant, bookkeeper, and other staff workers that would not be affordable for a sole owner.

What kind of person is suited to be a partner? All owners, but especially those who decide to have a partner or partners, should have the kind of personality not easily intimidated by the talents of others. Said another way, you should seek a partner who is as good as or better than you. *You must be willing to accept that this person is as good as or better than you!*

The second skill you'll need is the ability to trust. Notice again the similarity to marriage. You can't be looking over your partner's shoulder all the time. To the extent that your partner picks up on any mistrust on your part, it will influence her to begin to hide things. She may also return the mistrust in kind. Lack of trust and faith in the other partner is a sure path to disunity and the eventual demise of the partnership.

Moreover, one of you must be willing to give ground. It's even better if both partners possess this ability. At the same time, there can be only one head of any body, one ultimate authority. You have a better chance of winning the lottery than of running a successful business in which two or more partners have identical authority. This is not to suggest that there can't be a pure sharing of *power* fifty-fifty. It only means that each partner must have areas of authority where, when there is a dispute, one partner has the final say. The situation may be likened to the biblical approach to marriage where the two partners are completely equal, but the man is the head of the house. A critical element to remember about both the business and marriage partnership is that *the decision maker has the responsibility to make decisions in light of the other partner's needs. Otherwise, there is no trust!*

Finally, in a partnership situation, you must look for a balance of skills and thinking. There is far greater potential when partners bring varied skills and ideas to the table. If the owners are too much alike, it's possible to end up with redundancy that reduces the potential for productivity gains. Take, for example, a situation in which both partners in a law practice specializing in personal injury, both prefer to represent plaintiffs, and neither is particularly excited about management. It's clear that they haven't increased their potential client base through their association. Nor have they gained a critical skill—management—necessary to run a successful practice.

In the above example, it would make better sense to seek out a partner who has an interest in the management side of the business. A partner who was either a defendants' specialist in the same field of personal injury or who specialized in a different, though related, area would also be a good choice.

Part 1 The Spouse as Partner

It can and does work! Possibly you even know a couple who've had a wonderful forty years of marriage and also built a nice business together. But the pitfalls are numerous.

On the negative side, the couple will end up spending most of their waking hours together. The romantic says, "How can this be negative?" Reality tells us, though, that no matter how much two people like each other, there is a limit to how much time they can be together without driving each other nuts.

Dr. Joyce Brothers has said that it will help even strong

relationships if each spouse takes a full day off from the other every fourth day.

The strain is put on a married couple in a partnership situation simply because there are more reasons for conflict. It's one thing if you can limit your disagreements to how to spend the household budget or how to raise the kids. It's quite another if you must reach consensus on whether to expand into new markets or whether to fire Jennifer.

The positive side of the equation clearly outweighs the negative for the right couple. Involvement of both spouses gives each a complete view of the decision-making process, the ups and downs, and the pressures on the other spouse. There will be less question of who's making a contribution and fewer opportunities for distrust, especially since the opportunity for untrustworthy behavior is limited.

Another big benefit is that couples who share common goals have a significantly better chance of success in marriage. Starting a business is often equated with having a baby. The struggle of bringing a child to adulthood generally brings the parents closer together—so, too, with a business.

Who should try this approach? First, both spouses must genuinely love and respect each other. Second, there must be a clear line of command at home and an even clearer understanding of that line of command in the proposed new business. Like the partnership situation discussed above, equality of *power* is understood, but *authority* must be allocated.

Both partners must be able to make a real contribution. There can be big problems if one spouse feels that the contributions are unequal. That is not to say that they can't have greatly unequal skills or talents. However, each must feel that his or her skill or talent is truly needed by the firm and that both partners are giving a full effort. Surely this is true for partners who are not married. It's at least as critical, if not more so, for husband and wife.

Part 2 Other Family Members in the Business

The general rule: As much as possible, family members must be treated as well as, but not better than, other employees with the same position. This is for the family member/employee's benefit as well as for the benefit of the other employees. Favoritism has a way of cutting both ways; the morale of the other employees will be greatly affected, and those who are favored will be on the defensive about their privileged status.

Whether the family member is a cousin or dear old Dad, he'll be a better and happier employee, and you'll be a much happier employer if the ground rules are clearly established in the beginning and firmly enforced during the term of employment.

These general rules change very little if the family member is also a minority owner (has a smaller percentage of ownership than the largest shareholder, or partner). If you're to be the boss, you must be *the boss*. In you rests all authority, even that which has been delegated. Related partners may feel that because they have an investment and they are working in the business, they have special authority. If you agree to those strings in the beginning, so be it. (You'll regret it later, but then money does have its price.) You and your family member/partner will be better off, though, if you both agree that during the business day, he will be treated like anyone else—no better . . . and *no worse*.

Which brings us to another issue. Some family members are treated much worse than others in the business. A father may be trying to toughen up his son. A daughter may use the opportunity to give her mother as good as she got. A brother may continue a pattern of bullying that was present in the parents' home. These kinds of activities will be even more negative than the bestowing of privilege. They will create a great deal of tension that will pervade all the activities of an otherwise well-run company.

So, if you're going to bring your spouse or other relatives into the business as an employee or partner, do your best to leave the family relationship at the door. Conduct your office relationship in a business-like manner

.

CHAPTER

9

Part-Time Possibilities

I feel as if I could write an entire book on the part-time enterprise. There are millions of folks out there in the business arena making or losing a little money "on the side." Very few of these efforts are serious, and thus they are doomed to be no more than generators of loose change. The few people who are truly serious will suffer greatly from the failure to give their undivided attention just at the time when the business needs it most.

Here we'll deal only with the situation in which an individual starts a business on a part-time basis with every intention of going full-time as soon as there is enough business to justify leaving the old, paying job. While it's possible to start an enterprise this way (it's done all the time), this is by far the most difficult and risky method. It will be all-consuming of your time and energy, even beyond that of the full-time start-up, but it can work.

If you're thinking of taking this approach, ask yourself, "Is this really necessary? Could I work at my job a few more months and put aside enough money to start up full-time? If I wait and then devote one hundred percent of my personal resources to going out and getting clients, could I build the business fast enough to cover my overhead?"

If you honestly evaluate this question and still feel driven to

Start up part-time, you may want to consider the following types of businesses that lend themselves to that approach.

Some retail. Retail operations where personal service is not that important may allow you to hire unsupervised individuals to take care of the shop while you're at work. Ice cream parlors, card and gift shops, self-service gas stations, convenience stores, and others fall into this category. Certainly, you must have trustworthy help or incredible accounting systems to ensure that you are the sole beneficiary of each day's take.

Personal service businesses. A real estate agency, bookkeeping, consulting, selling advertising specialties, and leading seminars or self-improvement classes can all be pursued in the available time. This is not to say these enterprises wouldn't be better off with your undivided effort, only that they are better suited to a part-time launch than a barbershop or a real estate brokerage. Note how a real estate agency (listing and selling homes) is fine for part-time, whereas a brokerage (which employs agents, advertises listings, and so forth) is not.

Craft manufacturing. Tens of thousands of people create art or craft items that they sell to friends or at swap meets, art fairs, or on eBay. It's not such a big jump from earning a steady extra income through such a pursuit to then offering your bestsellers to retailers, wholesalers, mail order catalogs, or even major mass marketers.

Multilevel marketing. The pitch you'll hear from such multilevel marketers as Pampered Chef or Amway is that you can start part-time and work up to full-time. The fact is, it probably wouldn't pay to work at one of these enterprises full-time at first. You should, however, be willing to work just as hard at this as you would at a business in which you'd invested tens of thousands of your hard-earned, after-tax dollars. If you don't, you're not going to make more than pin money.

Franchises. Many franchises are designed to be managed by absentee owners. If you open a franchise while working your old job, make certain you have an understanding employer who'll let you take a few hours off here and there to handle emergencies. If you plop down fifty or sixty thousand dollars for a franchise, you're not going to want to feel awkward having to leave your "day job" to tend shop when your key manager has an auto accident.

10

Goal Setting and Success

There is a rule of thumb that those who write and speak about motivation, sales, and goal setting have all come to follow. These are not based on any study or science but are borne out by years of experience.

1. Only about 10 percent of highly motivated individuals who see themselves as on the fast track to success have a clear idea of what kind of financial future they want. In other words, they know they want to be successful but have only a vague idea of what that means to them.

2. Only a third of those have the guts to write it down. Somehow, this group knows intuitively that writing it down gives it a higher degree of meaning, including a greater degree of commitment as well.

3. Those who write down their goals are always at the top in earnings and accomplishments. They have clear ideas of what they want and are much more successful than those who go with the flow. Those who merely think about their goals do not achieve at the same level as those who commit goals to writing.

Part 1 A Personal Evaluation Project

If writing down clear goals and objectives is so important to future results, why don't those who desire to maximize their futures do so? Some don't know how. Some are afraid. Some just never slow down long enough to take the time. What follows is a comprehensive approach to self-evaluation and goal setting. If you take the time to carefully go through this process, you'll set yourself up for major success in anything you do.

What you're going to engage in here is a "personal inventory." It's not a test. There are no trick questions or trick answers. But it may be the most difficult assignment you've ever undertaken. In order to get useful results, it will be necessary for you to take a deep look into your own heart, soul, mind, and spirit.

It's imperative that you find a totally quiet place where you'll have no interruptions for at least two hours. I know this is hard in many homes, but if necessary, rent a hotel room, or find a secluded spot in the park.

HOW I SEE MYSELF

Take out a spiral notebook or other writing pad that you can keep forever. Open to page 1 and write at the top of the page: how I see myself. Now create two columns. On the left write positive. On the right, negative. Under positive, you should write a list of at least twenty positive things that you believe about yourself. Under negative, you should put the negative characteristics that seems to be the natural result of each positive item. The list might look like this:

HOW I SEE MYSELF: PART 1

POSITIVE	*NEGATIVE*
I am a happy person.	I can't relate to unhappy people.
I am an optimist	I am not always realistic
I have an even temperament	I never experience big highs or big lows
I have a good sense of humor.	I use it to gloss over serious issues
I am creative	I am absentminded
I am hard working	I don't tolerate those who aren't
I like to lead	I like to control others and the turn of events
I feel self-confident	I can be cocky
I make an excellent first impression	It commonly doesn't last.
I love my work	The parts I don't love I put off
I love God	I feel frustrated about not being spiritual enough
I like to develop things that have potential	I like to control people and events.

Now it's time to reverse the process. Begin first with the big negatives in your life. Write down at least ten. As you did above, now write the positives that might flow from these negatives. This second list might look like this:

HOW I SEE MYSELF: PART 2	
NEGATIVE	*POSITIVE*
I don't feel attractive.	I have done well with the opposite sex anyway.
I am opinionated.	My opinion is often sought.
I am very absentminded.	People look after me.
I am too competitive in noncompetitive arenas (discussion with spouse, etc.).	This is the same competitiveness that helps me in sports and business.
I haven't many good friends.	It is largely due to my attention to my family.
I dominate conversations.	I am an interesting speaker.
I am superficial in most relationships.	I am capable of giving some attention to many friends and associates.

I truly hope that you're now sitting in that secluded place with two hours to spare and your pen and notebook ready. If not, please don't go on. This is the time to put a place marker in the book and close it until you are in a position to do the above exercise.

It's human nature—and I am just as guilty as anyone—to look at the exercise just outlined and think such thoughts as: "I don't need to do that," or "I'll read on a little further and come back to this later," or "I wonder what he's driving at. I'll read on and check out the analysis first. Then I can decide whether I should take this test."

This is not a test. It is a very personal inventory of your feelings about your strengths and weaknesses. There is no grade and no cute list of what kind of person you are based on your answers. But if you'll go back and follow the directions to a T, you'll have your eyes opened up about who you really are. *Please! Stop reading now! Go back and do the exercise!*

With what I hope is not unfounded optimism, I'm assuming that at least 3 percent of you actually followed the most important piece of advice in this book and took a personal inventory. I use the 3 percent figure on purpose. The 3 percent who took the inventory is the same 3 percent who'll work through the rest of the exercises that follow. They're the very same 3 percent who'll eventually write down their goals. Yep! They're the 3 percent who'll do many, many times better than those who didn't have the courage to go through the self-analysis.

Now that you've completed the personal inventory, go back and take a look at all the negatives in both Part 1 and Part 2. Put a big 1 next to the negative that bothers you the most. Repeat this procedure for 2 and 3. Now put a line through those negative aspects that aren't that significant, or that you know you'll never consider changing. For the few that are left, decide whether they should have a #4 and so on, or if you should put a line through them.

Your chart should now look something like this:

HOW I SEE MYSELF: PART 1

POSITIVE	NEGATIVE
I am a happy person.	I ~~can't relate to unhappy people.~~
I am an optimist	I ~~am not always realistic~~
I have an even temperament 3	I never experience big highs or big lows
I have a good sense of humor.	I ~~use it to glow over serious issues~~
I am creative	I ~~am absentminded~~
I am hard working	I ~~don't tolerate those who aren't~~
I like to lead	I ~~like to control others and the turn of events~~
I feel self-confident 4	I can be cocky

I make an excellent first Impression	~~It commonly doesn't last.~~
I love my work 2	The parts I don't love I put off
I love God 5	I feel frustrated about not being spiritual enough
I like to develop things that have potential	~~I like to control people and events.~~

HOW I SEE MYSELF: PART 2

NEGATIVE		POSITIVE
I ~~don't feel attractive~~.		I have done well with the opposite sex anyway.
I ~~am opinionated~~.		My opinion is often sought.
I ~~am very absentminded~~.		People look after me.
I am too competitive in noncompetitive arenas (discussion with spouse, etc.).	6	This is the same competitiveness that helps me in sports and business.
I haven't many good friends.	7	It is largely due to my attention to my family.
I dominate conversations.	1	I am an interesting speaker.
I ~~am superficial in most relationships~~.		I am capable of giving some attention to many friends and associates.

What you've done above is to completely define yourself in your own eyes. If you've really thought about this in depth, your positives and negatives probably don't look anything like the above. Your list is probably longer, and maybe you've made some side notes.

You've also given yourself a blueprint for personal improvement. You've indicated those parts of your life that you'd really like to improve—parts about which you *care* enough to improve. The first rule of changing something about ourselves is that we have to want to make the change. Often, though, that list of negatives rolling around in our psyche is so ill-defined and so long that we don't want to think about changing any of it. What you've done here is sharpened the clarity of your list and shortened its length. You've made it manageable. Now it will be easier to make an improvement.

You've accomplished something else as well. By defining your negative attributes and then checking off those items that you don't care enough to change, you've greatly reduced your stress level. You've given these items up. You no longer have to carry them around with you.

On the positive side, you've admitted to yourself that you do have some wonderful characteristics. There are things about you that make you lovable, capable, and worthwhile. Now that you have a clear understanding of what your best features are, you can better direct the planning of your future. You can focus on the kinds of opportunities that will take advantage of those things you do best.

The next set of exercises is a bit easier than the last, but in some ways digs even deeper into the hidden parts of your being. If you've followed the instructions with regard to the above and have received the benefit that most do from taking the time and effort, you'll find that the same diligence applied to the following will yield similar benefits.

Once again, it's critical that you find two hours or so of quiet, uninterrupted solitude. You'll need your spiral notepad, pencil, and the same willingness to be open and honest with yourself. With these next exercises, you'll feel intense internal pressure to put down what society tells you-you should. Resist this with everything you possess. Put down your real feelings. You have nothing to lose and everything to gain.

As with the last exercise, please stop reading at this point until you are able to set aside the time to do it right.

THE LOTTERY

You come home from work and settle in to watch the evening news. You absently pick up your lottery tickets to see if you have any matches in this week's game. As the newscaster reads off the numbers you notice that you have two matches . . . then three, four, five, six, and even the bonus. You can't believe your ears or your eyes, but as the anchor-man repeats the numbers each and every one comes up the same as on your ticket. With equal parts of disbelief and excitement, you realize that you've just won three million dollars. After confirming the numbers with your spouse during the seven o'clock news, you begin to believe that it's possible.

After considerable shouting, dancing, and kissing, not to mention a few phone calls, you sit down to consider how you will spend this incredible surprise. That is the exercise that follows. However, unlike the real lottery, you've just been handed three million dollars in cash, tax-free. Write down the top ten things you would do with the money. (You don't have to stop with ten, but write down at least ten. Begin now. Don't read on.)

Wasn't that fun? Almost as fun as actually getting to spend it. Okay, not quite. Next, go back and put numbers next to each item in order of priority. In other words, #1 would be the item you'd want if you only had enough money to purchase one thing. Your ranking should have nothing to do with how much each entry costs. You have enough to purchase one thing. Make that #1. Now you have enough to purchase two things. Put a #2 next to the additional item you'd buy if there were enough funds for two. Continue this process up to at least ten.

Again, if you were thoughtful and honest about your selections, you probably have some new insights into who you really are. Let's go on to exercise four.

THE GENIE

You are out for a stroll along a totally secluded beach on the north shore of Oahu, Hawaii. You look down and notice a piece of brightly colored metal protruding through the sand. As you uncover it, you notice it is some kind of ancient lamp. As you brush the sand away, a genie appears from nowhere in a puff of smoke. (Feel like you've heard this story somewhere before?) The genie tells you that he is very grateful to you for releasing him from the lamp, and as a show of gratitude he will grant you three wishes. But you trick him; on the third wish, you ask for eight more wishes. He is outraged but has no choice but to comply.

Part of the bargain is that you have to tell the genie all ten wishes right now. Take up your pencil and paper and write down those ten wishes. If it isn't obvious to you already, these will probably be different from the lottery as they are not restricted to things you can buy. Do not read on until you have written down these ten wishes. If you wish to list more, you may.

If you haven't begun to have some new insights into your heart, soul, and mind by this time, you're either being dishonest with yourself or you're dead from the neck up. (There is one more possibility. You may be part of the three percent who know all this about themselves already.)

As with the lottery exercise, go back now and put numbers next to each entry in the order of their importance to you, without regard to their likelihood, cost, or any other criterion. Simply ask yourself which of these things would you most appreciate, which second, and so on.

Having done that, you should have just enough time left in your two hours to complete the following exercise.

THE ENCYCLOPEDIA

It is the year 2100. You're having a quick game of Super Mario Brothers 584 on your virtual reality video game set. You're doing this in heaven. You have long since passed away.

Saint Peter comes over to you and interrupts your play. He wants to send you on an important assignment down on earth. You agree and are instantaneously transformed into a librarian in Springfield, Illinois. You have plenty of free time on your hands as you begin your assignment. You decide it would be interesting to look yourself up in the Wikipedia and see what history has to say about you.

Beginning now, fill at least a full sheet of paper with what you'd want to find in the write-up of your life in Wikipedia many years after your demise. Think it through carefully. What would the article say about your career? Your family? Your contributions? Your admirers and detractors? Remember, this doesn't have to have anything at all to do with the life you're leading now. You're to write down what you'd *like* to find written about you.

As with the previous assignments, finish the exercise before continuing to read.

Wow! Are you getting excited yet? Is it time to take a serious look at how you have been conducting your life? Your two hours are undoubtedly up by now. If you have the time, you may wish to continue on into this next section. If you're out of time, you'll need to schedule a third two-hour slot for the final set of exercises.

If you're married, you may wish to have your spouse complete these same exercises. For you to have the best chance at creating a new beginning for yourself, you need to have your spouse along for the ride. Sure, there's a risk. When both of you are totally honest about these things, you may find out that you have many different desires and that your priorities don't match very well.

It's better that you both become aware of these differences, rather than keep these feelings to yourselves. How many partners are doing their best to attempt to make their spouses happy, when they're simply guessing as to what would truly make them so?

Once you each have an opportunity to discuss the hopes and dreams of the other, each of you can begin to share and take a bit of equity in the goals of the other. Once a person has some ownership, it is amazing how they begin to help rather than hinder their loved one in reaching the goal.

At this point, you need to be relaxed and alone. You should have with you your notebook and pencil, and be ready to be open and honest with yourself this one last time. If you're ready, read on.

Part 2 Setting Goals

Quickly reread what you've written under How I See Myself, The Lottery, The Genie, and The Encyclopedia.

Now put at the top of the page "my personal goals." Write down as many as you want, but make them realistic and make sure you're willing to sacrifice to attain them.

They can be big things like becoming the president of General Motors, or small things like losing ten pounds. They can be about any part of your life. They can be trips you want to take, children you want to have, or even the kinds of things you want for your kids or your spouse. You can list personality changes you wish to make or athletic achievements you want to pursue.

There is no time frame on these goals. Write them down even if you may not begin to attempt them for ten or twenty years. The longer-term goals are the more important ones.

Try to write fast and free. Don't be afraid to write down something you're not sure will stay on the list. You may want to try to put down twenty-five, fifty, or even one hundred items. There will be plenty of time later for revisiting this list and setting priorities.

Now is the time to stop reading and writing. Please don't read ahead until you have written down every goal you can think of.

You're now a part of that elite 10 percent that has given a great deal of thought to what it wants out of life. You fit into an in-between group that has also written down its goals. You're poised to be ten times more successful than those who have done neither. There are but three easy steps to take to join the very top three percent who have a clear set of written goals.

Part 3 Prioritize, Organize, and Internalize

First, prioritize. Go back over the list and put a 1 next to the item that is the most important to you, a 2 next to the second most important, and so on. As you're doing this, eliminate those items that you know you'll never attempt, or for which the reward just wouldn't be worth the effort.

Now organize. Create at least two lists: one for your career, and one for your home life. You may wish a third for your community aspirations. List your goals in priority order under each heading and leave about ten lines after each goal. Finally, create a brief outline under each goal showing what you'll have to do to accomplish the goal. For a final touch, put a date after each of the items, indicating the deadline you've set for the completion of each goal. Your page should now look something like this.

My Personal Goals

1. I want to be in a position to work or not work and not be concerned about the financial aspect of that decision by the time I'm fifty.

    A. I'll need to have $2 million in liquid net worth.

    B. I'll need to prepare myself for a life where work is not my life.

    C. I'll need to find a method for achieving the financial part in the twenty years I have left.

    D. I believe I can raise half of the $2 million through the sound conservative investment of 10 percent of my income each year.

    E. I believe I can raise the other half through the sale of an enterprise that I plan to open by the summer of next year.

2. I want to live in Hawaii on the island of Maui three months of every year, starting five years from now.

    A. My business will have to be able to get along without my presence; I'll have to be able to conduct business from there.

    B. I'll have to have the wholehearted support of my family and my business associates.

    C. I'll need to buy a condo or home within three years and arrange to rent it out the balance of the time I'm not occupying it.

3. I want all of my kids to reach adulthood without having tested drugs, become sexually active, and with their religious beliefs intact. I also desire that they all attend college.

    A. I must have my spouse's and kids' agreement in these goals.

    B. They should be written down by the kids as personal goals.

    C. I'll keep the kids in private schools where I can maximize my knowledge of—and input into—their schooling.

4. I want to lose fifty pounds in the next five months and keep it off.
   A. I'll have to select a weight-loss system within two weeks.
   B. I'll need to budget for the cost of that system.
   C. I'll have to ask for the cooperation of my spouse and family.
   D. I'll need to discipline myself to do an hour per day of exercise.

Business Goals

1. I want to build a business that will provide me with great personal satisfaction, $150,000-per-year income, and a salable asset worth $1 million in cash by the time I'm fifty.
   A. I must first decide exactly what business I wish to pursue.
   B. Then I must raise the necessary capital to open the doors.
   C. I must prepare myself with the skills to enter that business.
   D. I must work with my family to assure that everyone appreciates and agrees with my entrepreneurial choice. They must understand the potential sacrifices and how each of them will be affected.

2. I want to raise a minimum of $50,000 before I open the doors. If the venture that I choose requires more than that, I'll find a partner.
   A. I need to save $1,500 per month to reach that goal.
   B. I need to draw up a list of potential partners.

3. I want to have an impact on the industry that I choose. I'm not interested in merely providing a standard product or service. I want to do something new and different.
   A. I'll have to invest in knowledge of that industry in order to discern what is new and exciting, and what is not.
   B. I'll have to have the guts to go with my intuition.
   C. I'll have to pick an industry where my abilities will

allow me to have an impact.

4. I want to learn all I can about selling and computers before I open.

    A. I need to sign up for a computer class.

    B. I need to purchase a computer.

    C. I need to see if my current employer could use my potential computer skills.

    D. I need to purchase several books and tapes on selling.

If you've completed this section and feel good about what you've done, you have only one last step to take. You need to internalize your decision. You need to make it your own. You have to believe you can do it and dial in the desire to make it happen. How do you do that?

VISUALIZE

This time you need to find a quiet spot for only thirty minutes to an hour. Once you've done so, continue to read.

Lie down or get as comfortable as you can while sitting. Read over all of your material with special emphasis on your goals. Now, close your eyes and imagine the result of having achieved those goals. Think about every detail. What does it feel like to drive up to your own company in the morning and greet the employees who are supporting their families because of the jobs you're providing?

What does it feel like to produce products that you later see in the marketplace? Imagine, in detail, the excitement of landing your first really big contract or having to pay taxes on your first profitable year.

Take an imaginary walk on the sand in front of your home in Maui. Drink in the tropical breezes. Feel the warm surf on your bare feet.

It's a good idea to repeat this process very frequently. Your author finds himself indulging in this daydreaming (a sport for which I was roundly criticized as a child) just before falling asleep. I will think about even the most minute details of the steps in my overall goal and the excitement of reaching the summit.

Okay. Lie back and daydream. As usual, it's totally against the rules to read on until you've completed this exercise.

My heartiest congratulations to those of you who've completed each and every step. You still have a lot of work ahead of you. You'll have to show more discipline than you've ever shown before. But you're now positioned to be *one hundred times* more successful than the average member of your peer group.

A FEW MORE THOUGHTS ON GOALS

1.   They don't have to be grandiose to be meaningful. They need only be important to you.

2.   That you set a goal and fail to achieve it should in no way be seen as a failure. Setting a goal and not trying to achieve it. . . that can be considered failure.

3.   Goals are not set in concrete. There's nothing wrong with changing them as frequently as your situation changes. However, each change should be thoroughly considered.

4.   Publicize your goal. Tell your soulmates: your spouse, your best friend, and your partner. Some may be critical or jealous or sceptical. Your job is to use every comment made by these well-meaning associates to hone your goal. Even the least objective statements may have a kernel of substance that might help you to consider strategy changes.

5.   Don't let naysayers get in your way, though. There are two main reasons you're telling them your plans. One was covered in point 4. The other is that you'll be more motivated

to complete what you've started once you've told the world what you plan to do. Therefore, unless someone points out a fact that you truly hadn't considered before, let the negative folks have their say, and then move on.

6.   Make certain that you don't allow the goal to own you. You must own the goal. There are many things in this world that are well worth doing or having, but none of them is worth giving up your soul. You must be in control of your destiny. If you allow money, fame, or success in reaching your goals to take over your life, you'll end up being one miserable individual. Keep each part of your life in perspective, and you can find real happiness.

Enjoy a treasure trove of additional material on how to set and keep goals.

Useful books and websites on goals

Other personality tests for fun and personal analysis

All of these can be found by going to **https://WhenFridayIsntPayday.com** and looking for page 73

SECTION TWO

Opening the Doors

Note: Even if you have been in business for decades, the basic information contained in Section 1 will almost certainly still be hugely beneficial to you and your business. It is an easy read. Go back and check it out. You'll thank me later

.

1

Finalizing Goals

IF you've read through section 1, you understand the importance of goal setting. At this point you have probably set at least one goal: you intend to open a very small business that you expect will stay small. And you've probably selected the kind of business you intend to enter.

If you haven't yet made those two determinations, the following material will have very little meaning to you. If you're still undecided as to the type of enterprise, there's only one way to decide, and that's to research those that hold interest and make a decision. In going through the following exercises, you may change your mind about decisions you've already made. However, it's very unlikely that anything you read in this section will help to direct you to the first decision about enterprise type. You may wish to return to section 1 for some broad ideas of some available options.

Part 1 Establishing the Basic Blueprint

It's necessary at this point to fix on the details that will allow you to accomplish your goal. The questions below will help you create a solid business plan.

1.   What kind of business have you decided to enter? Be as specific as possible. For instance: "I intend to open a dog and cat hospital," as opposed to "I want to be a veterinarian." Another example: "I've decided to be a wholesaler of contemporary art prints," rather than "I'm going into the art business."

2.   By what date do you intend to open? Give an exact date.

3.   What are your primary motivations for starting this business? Some possibilities follow, but it's very important that you reach deep inside and find your own reasons. You'll very likely have more than one. Number these in order of importance.

> A.   Financial independence
> B.   Professional fulfilment
> C.   Independent work environment
> D.   Maximize personal potential
> E.   Exercise total control
> F.   Become famous
> G.   Prove something
> H.   Increase earnings
> I.   Create Wealth
> J.   Be accepted
> K.   Sell the new idea
> L.   Losing an existing job
> M.   Topped out in existing job
> N.   Special opportunity
> O.   Security

  P. Location not possible if employed

  Q. Pressure from ...

  R. Take over the family business

  S. Buy out present employer

  T. No choice (Why?)

 4. How much money per year do you desire to earn from your new business? First year_____ $ Second year $_____ Third year $_____ Fourth year $_____ Fifth year $_____

 5. What net worth do you wish the business to reach? By the end of the Fifth year $_____ Tenth year $_____ Twentieth year $_____

 6. By what other criteria will you judge the business to be successful? Again, here listed are some possibilities. Fill in your own.

  A. Leader in the field

  B. Dollar volume per year (list specific goals)

  C. Number of customers, clients, patients, etc. (be specific)

  D. Passing a going concern to my children

  E. Being recognized as an important concern

 7. As best as you can judge, which of the following elements are already in place and which will you have to obtain before you can open?

Element	Inplace	Not in place
Partners, if any	———	———
Finances	———	———
Education or training	———	———
Personnel	———	———
General location (city)	———	———
Family support	———	———

8. For each of the above, that is "not in place," select a deadline for putting that element in place. This will ensure meeting your timetable for the opening date above.

You've now established a basic blueprint for action. Now it's time to make certain that you're not so wrapped up in your business goals that you've forgotten the rest of your life.

The following questions may remind you of some that you've seen before in section 1.

1.   What are your top three personal goals for your lifetime?

2.   Indicate the times by which you hope to achieve each of these goals. For instance:

A.   My most important goal is to reach financial independence for my family. I define this as having a liquid net worth, not including my personal residence of $1 million. I hope to achieve this by my fortieth birthday.

B.   My second most important goal is to create a family environment that will result in my spouse and me enjoying a lifetime of marriage together, and my children reaching adulthood with a minimum of pain for them and us. This goal does not have a completion date as such, but the result should be fairly clear by the time my youngest is eighteen.

C.   My third most important goal is to provide a lasting contribution to my community. My plan at this time is to open a small group home for troubled youth. I'd hope to achieve this about the time my youngest leaves home.

3.   Of course, your goals look far different from these, but they give you a possible approach for constructing them. The next question becomes: Are any of your business goals in direct contradiction to your personal goals? If they're in perfect harmony, you're a very fortunate individual. If not, now is the time to resolve any differences.

One way to resolve them is to eliminate one or the other of the conflicting items. Many individuals who have the energy to consider the life of an entrepreneur also find that they have so many goals that there's constant conflict. There not enough hours in the day to create a great little business, give plenty of love and devotion to the family, be a pillar of the community, be active in three or four sports activities, and still find time to write a novel. Thus it may be necessary to give up one or more of these ideas.

Another method is to put off something that can wait. I've had the goal of taking a year off to travel and gather my thoughts. This is a dream that will have as much validity in ten years as it has today but will be far more practical then than now.

You may merely wish to modify some of the conflicting plans. Becoming the best golfer at your club within five years could take huge amounts of time away from your business just when it needs you most. Moving the date of your goal to ten years may allow you to devote single-minded attention to your business for the first five years, after which you can begin your run at golf greatness.

Part 2 Three-Track Thinking

A final thought as you put the finishing touches on your life plan. There are many components that go into determining whether you can maintain your equilibrium while undertaking a challenge as great as business ownership. One of these I call "three-track thinking."

There are those who would advise you to set a single course and stick to it no matter what happens. That advice is appropriate for your marriage, but not for the very small business. You need to keep your options open and close at hand. For example, You've just decided to open a computer business specializing in computer repairs. You have three years' experience with this type of work and believe that you can run the business out of your home. You've begun to accumulate the needed equipment and your current employer has announced plans to close up his operation and retire in three months.

It would be natural and normal for you to assume that you'll just take over his customer base, keep your overhead low, and enjoy good profits from day one. Unfortunately, one week before you open, your old boss loses half his wealth in an uninsured apartment fire, and he is forced to stay in business.

If you're a one-track thinker, your old boss's decision will cause you much despair. The pie will be cut in half at best. At worst, you may be unable to capture any of the business loyal to your ex-employer. In addition, you feel a certain loyalty to your boss and feel uncomfortable competing with him.

Three-track thinking works like this. When you make the decision to open a computer repair store, you also consider other similar kinds of repairs. In this case that might include a different specialty (Apple) or a different electronic product (smartphones, copiers). You also research the customer base for computer repairs beyond your current company's customer list. Finally, you investigate other employment opportunities as an ultimate backup.

Being prepared with plan A, B, or C doesn't mean that it will be completely painless when an unexpected roadblock appears. It does mean that you'll sleep better at night knowing that you do have options.

It's possible and desirable to use three-track thinking in almost everything you do in virtually every area of your life. This method of dealing with life's little surprises is particularly useful when you have a hint of a storm brewing. However, the expert practitioner will have one or more parallel tracks to divert to for every important aspect of his business.

CHAPTER

2

Preparing the Business Plan

It's possible to open and operate a successful new enterprise without first preparing a formal business plan. It's also possible for a brain surgeon to successfully remove a malignant tumor from your skull without first having an MRI and spending hours in consultation to determine how to do the job. But would you want that doctor operating on you? If the answer is no, then you also don't want to have someone running your business who hasn't gone to the same trouble and more to prepare for that job. The someone we're talking about is you.

The business plan is not just a document to look at later to make certain you've followed a certain path. It's more a method of thinking through each aspect of your business in an attempt to work through as many problems as possible before they occur. You may, indeed, find it instructive to refer to your plan from time to time after you're open to see if you've forgotten an important aspect or taken an unintended direction. The real value, however, is in the preparation.

Most of the rest of chapter 2 is devoted to a series of questions to which you should know the answers long before you open your doors. Each question is accompanied by commentary designed to help you make decisions about that question. In many cases, you'll need to do research in order to respond properly. The more thought, calculation, and research that you invest in this section, the greater the chances for a successful launch of your new enterprise.

Part 1 The Business Purpose

Until now you've been thinking about goals, hopes, and dreams having to do with your personal life and career. From this point forward you will need to *shift your thinking.* You're now the president, chairman of the board, and senior partner of a separate, legal entity. (No, I haven't skipped ahead. Even though you haven't yet created this business, you should begin thinking as if it were already in existence.)

As the leader of this new concern, it's your primary responsibility to steer your ship on a course that is most likely to get it safely to harbor. Now you must concentrate on the needs of the business. *These are likely to be different, though hopefully not at odds, with your own specific goals.*

For instance, the primary reason you may have started the business is to achieve economic independence. It's unlikely that the best goal of the *business* is to make *you* independently wealthy. The goal of the business is more likely to be selling the most widgets possible at a price that will allow you to cover overhead and make a profit.

Your personal goal may be to retire by age forty. Your reason for going into business may be to have an outlet for your creative energy. You can be certain that if the purpose of your business is to achieve either of those ends, you're destined for failure. A more appropriate business goal might be to provide very-high-quality print services to local businesses at bargain prices.

With that lengthy introduction out of the way, it's time to create your business purpose. Here are questions to help you to define it. As with the exercises in section 1, you'll benefit most if you write out the answers to each of these questions *now*.

1. What product or service will you be providing? Be specific. Rather than "the grocery business," say "convenience store with gas pump." Instead of the general category of "law practice," say "general legal practice with a specialty in personal injury."

2. At what level in the distribution chain will you be? Manufacturer, wholesaler, jobber, rep, retailer, business to business, or other?

3. Describe your quality and pricing approach. A few examples might be:

   A. Cutthroat prices on commodity products until I'm established, and then increase to industry norm.
   B. Highest-quality products with prices to match.
   C. Unique products that should command prices slightly higher than competition.
   D. Service and quality will be as good as anyone's, but specializing in discounting and volume.

The list could go on and on. What is your approach going to be?

4. What geographic boundaries describe your territory? Also, indicate whether this is by choice or imposed by contract. For instance, a retail business may figure it can reach a five-mile radius. A wholesaler may be expecting to reach a three- or four- state area. A manufacturer may see the world as his oyster (though the manufacturer's rep may be limited by her contract to a certain area). A manufacturer may have licenses that restrict his selling area. A franchisee almost certainly has certain boundaries beyond which he may not offer his product or service.

5. *What special niche do you plan to fill?* This is one of the most important questions you will answer in section 2. That being the case, we will now take a brief detour to look at this issue in detail.

The dictionary defines a niche as, "A place suitable for a person or thing." As part of your mission statement, you'll want to find the place in the field you're entering that is suitable for you. However, you'll have much greater success if you take the concept of "niche" one step further. You'll want to find a place that is unique, separate, and distinct from others providing similar goods or services.

Why is this so important? Because it will give you something to talk about when you're selling your product. Because it will allow' you to charge more than the competition if you can find a need that is not currently being met. Because it will give you an opportunity to become the "leader" in that specific way of doing business. And, as we'll show later, leadership is a big asset to a company.

You don't have to have a niche to be successful. If you're a super-successful salesperson and plan to function as a manufacturer's representative, you'll probably do just fine if you can find a few good factories to represent. You might really become something special, however, if you offer those same factories representation in India besides your normal three-state territory. That would be a special niche.

You might think that a doctor would be hard-pressed to come up with a niche. How about opening at 6:00 a.m.? Or making house calls? One of my friends made a small fortune as one of the first doctors to specialize in sports medicine.

In other words, if everyone else is selling price, sell service. If your competition is well known for quality and service, but his prices are out of line, come in with some really hot pricing. If the rest of the market is selling your product in basic black, offer yours in color. If color is the current rage, you may find that your customers would love to eliminate inventory and go back to black.

Potentially you can create a niche out of almost any element of your business. Does anyone currently sell what you sell by phone? How about by e-mail, eBay, or through a Web site? Do other manufacturers sell your product only to distributors? Maybe you should try selling it directly.

Packaging, advertising strategy, promotions, even an informative email newsletter can set you apart from all the others.

One of the best niche plays of all is to have protected merchandise. That is, to have products or services that no one else can sell due to the protection of patents, trademarks, copyrights, or proprietary information. One of the companies I used to manage would only rarely consider a new product line that wasn't protected by one of these devices.

For instance, if your competition is selling a notebook for $1.99 and it has a plain yellow cover on it, you may be able to sell an identical notebook for $2.49 just because it has a cute picture of a famous, lasagna-loving cat on the front. Sure, you'll have to pay a royalty for that, and it may cost a few cents extra for the four-color cover. However, the difference won't come close to the normal margin of profit on $2.49, and no one else will be able to offer that notepad to your customer. In reality, you'll have created a mini-monopoly.

One of my companies was once selling a bicycle security cable that every competitor in town also carried. We asked the manufacturer to make one for us that was one foot longer and to restrict his sales of that product to our company since we'd suggested the idea to him. We then showed our customers that this extra foot was a benefit. Within a few weeks, we'd sewn up almost all the business in that product. We'd created a niche.

Your special niche doesn't necessarily have to be highly creative. Maybe you're just the best there is at your task. Another of my friends decided to make some extra money hanging wallpaper. There was nothing special about her part-time business, except that she was immensely talented at installing wallpaper. With very little effort she was soon swamped with business.

Unless you're quite certain that you can build a reputation around your special skills, don't count on craftsmanship alone. Possibly my friend's wallpaper venture would have even grown faster had she also let the word out that she could finish any job within forty-eight hours. When people decide to paper their home, they want it done *now*. This could have been a very successful niche.

A classic niche is "filling a void" in the marketplace. In 1989 the company I headed began producing bicycle water bottles. No one was manufacturing a water bottle in the United States for sale to the wholesaler. Those that were being produced domestically were sold directly to retailers. Our customers were having to purchase their water bottles from Taiwan and Europe. By filling this void we were able to capture close to half of the business in our market the first year.

Our overwhelming success in water bottles wouldn't have been possible if there'd been other manufacturers making bottles for the wholesaler. We moved into the niche and saturated it. With our domination of the category, we've also made it very difficult for a competitor to move into our territory.

Many businesspeople have opened their doors believing that a great location is all that is needed to bite off a chunk of the market. Although location can be extremely important to the success of certain business types, only rarely does this element alone propel a business to success. For instance, owning a food concession at an airport or ballpark may be a great niche, but you still won't be the only concessionaire. You'll still need to offer something special to get folks to come to your stand.

There's no reason you can't have more than one niche. Every additional successful niche you find will make your business grow and prosper. Let's return to the example of the doctor. He might build an incredible practice by specializing in sports medicine, getting a famous athlete to endorse his clinic, and producing a newsletter that offers tips for preventing injury.

As a final example, let me tell you about one of the greatest niche players I've ever seen. There is a nationwide chain of grocery outlets known as Trader Joe's. Trader Joe's concept fits our definition perfectly. In this day of grocery stores that are larger than football fields and offer thousands of items, Trader Joe's are usually under ten thousand square feet and sell little else than gourmet items including beer and wine.

The story doesn't end there. Many of the wines have been specially purchased by the company. They might buy all of a given lot, and then put Trader Joe's brand on the label. Next, they hand out or mail out a newsletter about the wine that has been specially chosen, and that you can only buy at Trader Joe's.

There's more. They do the same thing with cheeses and with products as diverse as peanut butter and ice cream. Oh! Lest I forget, the original owner, Joe, developed such a reputation for his knowledge of wine and cheese that he was asked to do short segments about these topics on the local radio in Los Angeles, where the franchise started. You can only imagine the value of those free spots on Los Angeles radio programs.

What will there be about *your* business that will *set you* apart? Why will your potential customer arrive at your door rather than your competitor's? What is so special about your offer that you'll be able to take business away from others who've been in business for decades?

A final secret about niches. You may not have to continue to offer this special approach forever. Frequently, after building his business to a certain level, a price discounter will begin slowly to raise the price. Special hours may begin to be trimmed back. Less profitable products or services might be eliminated.

You must be careful when you do this. You don't want to kill the goose that laid the golden egg. You'll also want to make certain that you're still giving your customers a very good reason to trade with you instead of your rivals. This could even mean establishing a new niche to replace the old. For now, however, as you prepare to open your doors, develop as many unique approaches to offer your customer in product and/or service as you can think of. There may be an expense associated with some of these. Therefore, you'll want to weigh the expense against the expected benefit. Of course, you must also weigh the expense against your ability to pay.

Now is the time. Write out each and every special niche you will occupy.

After you've answered the preceding five questions, you should be prepared to write out your formal statement of business purpose, or mission statement. This should be a concisely written description of your overall approach. It may be only one sentence. It surely shouldn't be more than three.

As an example, here's a mission statement for one of the companies I helped establish, AC International: "AC International is a marketing company that manufactures for sale to wholesalers and mass retailers a line of high-quality, unique, protectable bicycle accessories that enhance the bicycling experience."

The first thing you notice about this statement is that AC International is a marketing company. The company may be a manufacturer as is stated in the next phrase, but the emphasis is on marketing, not manufacturing. It would be just as easy for a company to be successful with that phrase reversed: "ABC Company is a *manufacturer* that *markets* for sale . . However, these two companies would be as different as night and day.

The marketing company emphasizes product design, packaging, methods of distribution, and advertising. The manufacturing aspect of its business is a part of the overall marketing strategy. The company may be manufacturing in order to achieve lower cost, control over delivery of the finished product, or protection of trade secrets.

In contrast the manufacturing company orients itself toward certain types of manufacturing capability. It then looks for markets where its capacity can be sold. It will usually do only enough marketing to move product out the door, and its customers to provide packaging, advertising, and distribution.

The next phrase simply states who the customers are.

The final line describes the niche. Our company seeks products that are unlike any other. These items should be protectable by patents, trademarks, copyrights, or proprietary knowledge. The product category is bicycle accessories. AC International is not dividing its attention into other areas.

Last, we laid out our goal of "enhancing the bicycling experience." This slogan appeared on our advertising and packaging. It's how we wanted to be perceived by our customers. We weren't merely selling any product that comes along. We wanted to make a statement with these products.

Your mission statement may have all of these elements, only some of them, or you may say it in a totally different way. There's no right or wrong way to put down these ideas. The two important things are (1) that you write down a mission statement and (2) that you think about this statement so thoroughly that you can say it in one or two sentences.

You will receive far more benefit from the rest of this section on creating a business plan if you've written out your mission statement. It's possible that you'll change your original statement by the time you've finished section 2. You may also revise it further as you move toward your opening date. There's a good likelihood that it will change again after you've been open a while. However, as was the case with your goals, the fact that this statement may change does not invalidate the reasons for going through the process of developing it.

Write out your mission statement now.

Part 2 Finding a Location

Much of what you've accomplished until now has been done in your mind and on a piece of paper. Next, we begin to attack those elements that will require research, fieldwork, and interaction with others.

Location is a critical factor for retail stores, personal services, and restaurants. Don't, however, underestimate the importance of site selection for many other businesses.

You should be prepared to spend more time, money, and energy on this issue than almost any other. Recently, a friend wanted to open a clothing store. She believed she'd located a great storefront and entered into negotiations for a lease. While this was going on, she started making purchases of the next season's fashions.

Unfortunately, negotiations broke down on that store. She immediately started looking for an alternative. The clothing she'd purchased would be delivered in sixty days. With so little time she was forced to compromise. She took a marginal store that had poor parking access and no foot traffic. Six months later, she had a stack of bills and no business.

The following are criteria to consider in selecting a location. Some of these may not apply to your type of business. Even so, carefully evaluate each one.

TRAFFIC

On the surface, this would seem to be the most obvious issue of all. Now let's take a look below the surface.

Certain kinds of businesses can benefit from traffic, vehicular and/or pedestrian. Your decision-making process must take into consideration: (a) Do you need traffic? (b) What kind? (c) How much rent are you willing to pay for various levels of traffic? (d) How do you maximize your location's advantage to bring the traffic into the store?

Most businesses open to the general public can benefit from traffic. By contrast, businesses who cater to a limited clientele or who have no reason for customers to walk in shouldn't pay extra for a location that offers good traffic.

Many service providers such as doctors, lawyers, advertising agencies or auto insurance brokers seem to think that the prestige of a top-floor office in the town's tallest building is best for them. They might find that they'd attract quite a bit of walk-in traffic if they were to relocate in a ground-level storefront on Main Street.

There are many different types of traffic. If you were interested in opening a sandwich shop, you'd want to have a location where many clerical workers and middle managers would see you. Executives and factory workers don't go to sandwich shops. Neither do Mom and the family.

If you're opening a fancy restaurant, you probably don't want to locate in an industrial center. You need traffic at night to fill up your restaurant, and industrial areas turn into tombs at night. You want to be where middle- and upper-class folks can see you and get to you conveniently for dinner. This might mean a corner strip mall in an upscale residential area, an area that features other nighttime entertainment, or an upscale shopping center.

Yours is not the only business that wants to maximize certain kinds of traffic. Where there is competition for a scarce commodity, those who desire that commodity must be willing to pay a premium to get it. Your next decision is: How much extra money for how much extra traffic?

I wish I could give you a wonderful mathematical formula for determining how to make this decision. I haven't seen one, nor can I imagine how to derive one. Advertising is similarly vague. You know it will benefit you, but it's very hard to know how much to spend.

If you depend on foot traffic, I don't think it's possible to underestimate the importance of the quality and quantity you need. Being on the second floor of a second-rate mall will be death for your ladies' shoe business when there are three others on the first floor. However, you might survive on the second floor if yours is the only vitamin store in that mall.

Vehicular traffic is a harder call. A fast-food restaurant

might have an almost exactly proportional volume of business to the volume of traffic. Knowing this, it might negotiate the lease accordingly. A furniture store competing for the same location may not be able to expect an exactly incremental increase based on pure traffic. They may have to rely more on the internet, TV, and mailers to produce customers.

If traffic is a consideration, you'll want to learn as much as you can about the type of traffic you can expect at the various locations you are considering. A shopping center manager will usually have figures. An industrial real estate agent will usually have numbers supplied by his client. *Get your own!*

Buy an inexpensive counting device, go to the location, and count. Stop people and take a short survey. Those folks who're willing to stop will give as much as five or ten minutes of their time. You'll want to determine who they are, why they shop here, and whether they have any need for what you'll be offering. You'll need to survey at least a hundred people for the results to have validity.

PROXIMITY TO CUSTOMERS

If you rent used cars to people whose auto is in the repair shop, you'll want to locate your business near auto repair shops. This may seem obvious. Less obvious might be this example. If you're a wholesaler selling locksmith supplies to lock and key shops in a five-state area, where do you locate to be close to your customers?

After some investigation (including asking your future customers' advice) you'd probably decide to locate in the traffic center of a large urban area. Why? Locksmiths often need product *today*. If you're located an hour away and your competitor is two hours away (in the suburbs where the rent is lower), you're going to get the job. As this customer comes to rely on you for the rush job, you're likely to get his regular business as well.

A manufacturer which sells to wholesalers has no reason to be close to customers. Others who fall in this category would be mail-ordered companies, import-export companies (they may need to be close to a port), or television production companies.

NEIGHBORHOOD

Shopping for a business home is in many ways like shopping for a home for your family. You'd prefer to be in a nice, clean, crime-free environment. There are advantages to being close to needed services such as restaurants, print services, office supply stores, and the post office. Where is your source of employees? Their needs may play a part. You may want to be near certain kinds of recreation or within a certain commute time. You hope you'll never need it, but it may be worth a few extra dollars per month to be near police and fire services.

Some of the above may be critical. Is your customer going to come to a known high-crime area just to do business with you? Will you have difficulty attracting the kind of employees you need if the commute time from that kind of residential area is an hour or more? If you plan to project a high-tech image, will you be able to overcome a low-tech neighborhood? What about the neighbors? A little bit of research might show you that the arcade on the corner is going to attract certain clientele that will not help your business. If you're going to be in an industrial area, are there neighbors who might create environmental concerns? I used to live next to an agricultural college. When the wind blew in the wrong direction . . . need I say more? Noise, odors, unsavory visitors, bitter contests for available parking, and dangerous activities are a few of the things you may want to be on the lookout for before signing a long-term lease.

GOVERNMENT AND LOCATION

Local governments are not all alike. Some are quite enthusiastic about business. Others are downright inhospitable. You may be the type of person who naturally follows all the rules to a T, enjoys working with government employees, and filling out forms. If you are, you're not the typical entrepreneur.

When I was in the rental car business, I had two locations. Each had an office trailer, a sign, and a space to do minor repairs. In one city, we were able to open without any permit other than a business license, which took half an hour to secure.

In the other city, we had to have a variance to be in the rental car business at all. Our sign was not in adherence to code, for which we were cited within six weeks of opening. The trailer also required a variance, and we were told the two-year variance would not be renewed. We would have to arrange to build a permanent structure within two years.

A good industrial real estate agent should be able to tell you something about the government attitude toward your enterprise type in the various cities you're considering.

PARKING

Several times, I've seen friends and associates open in locations where parking was a clear problem. "Oh," they assured me, "it may affect business a little, but the rent is cheap. Besides, look at this visibility." The rent was cheap because there was no parking. The result in every case was a disaster.

Now that you know some of the elements that go into the decision about location, how do you go about finding the perfect spot?

Here comes another one of those golden nuggets: *Use a commercial real estate broker*

Yes, there's a chance you could save a few bucks by dealing directly with a landlord who doesn't have to pay a commission. But there's a greater likelihood that the landlord may try to take advantage of you without a real estate agent there to help you.

You find a commercial real estate broker the same way you find any other service provider. Start with networking. Then try the Internet and the local chamber of commerce. Interview several brokers. Each one will provide you with invaluable information about current market conditions. Some may have differing opinions. The combination of those opinions can be quite eye-opening.

Like all agents, commercial real estate agents will stress how important it is that you deal with just one. They will provide great arguments about how everyone has access to the same listings. They'll tell you how embarrassing it is to have two different agents making inquiries about the same property for the same client.

Forget it. Let them think they're exclusive if it will make them feel better, but you should have at least two agents working. No one can have complete knowledge of anything so complex as the commercial real estate market for a given area. Even within a small geographic area, different agents have brought me vastly different options when they've been presented identical criteria. You need all the information you can possibly get for this important decision. Use two agents.

If two is better, is three best? Maybe. There probably is a point of diminishing returns, but until I've located an excellent property, I continue to interview new agents. I may not actually send more than two or three out looking, but I keep my options open.

As we'll discuss later, always remember that the commercial real estate agent is usually also working for the landlord. The agent has certain responsibilities of disclosure due you, but you must maintain a certain wariness at all times.

Remember, also, the experience of my friend with the

clothing store. Have a backup location in mind until you sign the lease, and don't make other irreversible decisions.

Once you've selected your location, write it up in your business plan. List the strengths and weaknesses. What do you expect the location to do for your business? What were your reasons for selecting it? What are the drawbacks that you hope to be able to overcome? How will you take advantage of the positive aspects of this site?

Before we leave this area, let's evaluate the last question. You've worked hard, analyzed the choices, and you can't imagine having picked a better spot for your new enterprise. You're a CPA specializing in corporate taxes and you're located right next door to the biggest corporate law practice in town. Maybe you're opening a specialty bookstore, and you've taken a lease on the closest retail store to a major campus. Maybe your location stinks, but the rent on your restaurant is the envy of every other restaurant owner in town.

Your work, location-wise, has just begun. The CPA could merely hope people will see his name on the door as they come to visit the attorney. Or, he could go next door and work out some deals with his neighbor. The neighbor might agree to something as simple as leaving business cards on the reception desk, or something as complex as selling each other's services.

Let's look at the specialty bookstore situation. The owner will not maximize her extra expense for the rent on that incredible location if she merely puts up an attractive sign. She needs the nicest sign ever. As big as the local law will allow. She should also consider a sandwich board on the sidewalk, sidewalk sales every day, and/or students handing out fliers in front of the store to maximize the advantage she's paying for.

And what about our restaurateur who's accepted cheap rent instead of a great location? He should have the extra money to rent the largest and best-located billboard in town to tell folks who he is and where. He should offer to those who find him a free meal each time they return and bring a new friend along.

Taking into consideration all of those elements, including the excellent attributes that you are paying extra for, and the negatives that you may need to overcome, add to your business plan the methods you can think of to take advantage of your great new site.

Part 3 Selecting Suppliers

Who will supply you? If your business will be primarily aimed at supplying product rather than services, nothing is more important than your sources of supply. Most service providers must pay attention to supply as well. However, the products and services they must purchase are usually widely available and very price competitive.

For example, an electric scooter rental company will need to purchase the scooters, and will certainly need phone, specialized apps, and communication equipment. It will also need repair services. The quality and cost of each one of these could substantially affect the profits of the company, but each of these items can be readily purchased from other suppliers if necessary.

Most retailers, on the other hand, build up certain brand names and become known by the brands they carry. If that major vendor has supply problems, does not maintain a competitive posture in the marketplace, or cuts you off due to poor performance or bad credit, you could be out of business in short order.

Wholesalers, importers, and many manufacturers are in the same position. One manufacturing company I know of had been in business just three years when the raw material required to make their only product was discontinued by a major chemical company. They believed that it was the only product that would work. It had been part of the formula that accompanied the manufacturing instructions when they took over the company. They were *panic-stricken!*

Fortunately, they were able to find another source, but they were out of production for almost a month in the middle of their season. This happened, of course, just as they were finally turning the corner on profitability.

I could provide you with a list of such instances from my personal experience, and then another one ten times as long from the experiences of friends and acquaintances. Golden nugget: It's the opinion of this author that **suppliers are more important than customers**. I have a saying that I pass on to my employees and associates: "Customers are easy; vendors are hard!"

Let me give you an example from my own business. As mentioned before, AC International made bicycle water bottles. They were top quality. Our price was right. And our customers wanted us to supply them. We didn't need to *sell* any bottles. Our customers were lined up to get them.

Initially, we were going to buy all of our bottles from a job shop. This manufacturer said he could make 150,000 bottles per month. We took orders for that many. Our supplier delivered only 40,000 the first two months, and we were no longer in the business of taking orders for bottles. We were now in the business of handling customer complaints. Not only were we failing to realize the sales we could have had in those months, we were making our customers angrier by the day. Additionally, we were opening the door wide for competition to take advantage of our inability to ship.

Your suppliers can make you or break you. You'll have to select many of your most important suppliers before you even open your doors. How do you make a good judgment about this critical issue?

Product vendors are generally judged on four criteria: quality, price, delivery, and terms. It's rare that you'll find suppliers that will rate at the top of their class on all four. Thus, you'll have to make trade-offs and arrive at the optimum for your kind of business.

For instance, if you're in a one-man auto repair shop, you must be able to get any part for the one car you're working on in one day. You care about price, but you'll gladly pay a good bit more to get it today rather than next week.

The wholesaler of televisions to local TV retailers will probably be more concerned about the terms he gets from the manufacturer. It will be very expensive for him to maintain a large inventory of TV sets. He may continue to carry a line that has some quality problems if he gets ninety days to pay.

It's time for you to come to a few conclusions for your own enterprise. In this part of your business plan we'll deal only with suppliers who provide goods and services that are integral to the product or service you'll be selling.

1. Rate the four criteria by which vendors are judged on a scale of 1 to 10. For instance: Quality 9; Price 10; Delivery 6; Terms 8.

2. Now take each of your top four products or services and rate the vendor performance that you need for each. An example of a bicycle shop might look like this:

Bicycles: Quality 8	Price 8	Delivery 9	Terms 9
Clothing: Quality 10	Price 7	Delivery 7	Terms 9
Locks: Quality 9	Price 7	Delivery 8	Terms 6
Tools: Quality 10	Price 5	Delivery 5	Terms 6

3. Some or all of the products, services, or raw materials you need may have very limited sources of supply. Make a list of those items that you believe may be available only from one source. For example, when I owned the used car rental business, there was only one insurance company in the United States that was insuring used rental cars. That was an important negative in my business plan.

4. Is there anything you need where it would be important to have a name-brand supplier? If you'll be selling computers, can you make it without Dell or Apple? Make a list of these situations.

5. Now begins some very hard work. Begin to compile a list of companies that could provide you with the needed resources for your business. Use the Internet, industry magazines, buyers' guides, and trade associations; the local chamber of commerce; U.S. Department of Commerce listings; and every other method you can come up with to prepare a comprehensive list.

6.   Begin with the most important product. Get on the phone. Call the company and ask to speak with a salesman. *Do not write a letter asking for information and do not use the e-mail on the "contact us" page of their Web site;* either will get lost in the shuffle. The salesman is the guy who stands to gain the most from your new account. Tell him you're getting ready to open in his territory and you'd like to get together for breakfast some morning.

Why breakfast? It won't take him away from his selling day. Use the breakfast to find out whether his territory has any neighborhoods where his product is not getting enough exposure. Learn all you can about the strengths and weaknesses of his company. Find out what it takes to qualify for credit terms, and how much merchandise he thinks you'll need to open up your operation.

See if he'll introduce you to a couple of his best accounts— ones that are located far enough away from your territory that you wouldn't represent a competitive threat to them.

If possible, try to arrange a tour of the supplier's facilities, and an opportunity to meet the salesperson's superiors. Even the owner.

Without waiting for your first choice of supplier to implement all this, move on to other potential suppliers and repeat the process with as many as you have time for. The more of this you do, the more likely you will be to secure vendors that can help make your business.

7.   In the case of those companies that don't have field representatives, and that is too far away to visit in person, have them send you all the information possible. Also, don't be afraid to take the time to gain as much information over the phone as you can.

8.   Create a notebook where you write down extensive notes on your visits. Start a library of the catalogs, brochures, and price lists that you pick up along the way.

9. By now you've surely begun to make certain decisions about your primary suppliers. Write up each one in your business plan. Indicate what they'll supply and describe their strengths and weaknesses.

10. Where necessary or desirable, enter into formal contracts with your preferred suppliers. Indicate in your business plan the contracts you've secured and what the terms are.

Some of your preferred vendors may not be prepared to supply you. They may have territory problems. They may not be inclined to sell to new businesses. They may not like your credit standing. If you run into this situation, and you feel it's important to have this supplier as a part of your team, you'll need to turn into a salesperson.

It's the rare occasion where a good salesperson won't be able to persuade a company to sell him or her their product. That's not to say that anyone can get a McDonald's franchise in a location where contracts and covenants preclude it, but most situations aren't that cut and dried.

Selling yourself to a vendor isn't that hard. What they want from you is simple: high sales volume and fast payment. If you can convince the decision maker that you'll give them these two things, you'll seldom have any trouble getting the lines you need.

Generally, the vendor salesperson has the power to decide whether or not you become a customer. The credit department will take over when it comes to whether or not you'll get credit, and how much you'll get. If you've selected a vendor that you think may be tough to sell, call the salesperson again to set up another breakfast.

Begin your discussion by assuming his willingness to sell to you, unless you know that this meeting is to overcome his decision not to. Ask questions that would imply that you'll be doing business together: "If I give you an order today for seventeen hundred widgets, when can I expect delivery? Has your credit department had a chance to examine my credit application yet? Will you waive the freight on my first order?"

If the salesperson balks at this approach and says that he's either unsure of adding you as a customer or not inclined to, it is time to begin selling. Enthusiasm is all important. At this point, enthusiasm is all you have. You can't prove your ability to move mountains of product, and you have no track record for paying your bills. Bring to the fore every bit of excitement you can muster and make this person believe he's going to make money with you. You are going to feature his product in your store, in your brochures, on your Web site, and in your email blasts. You'll carry a full range of his product, not just cherry-pick the line. You might even offer to carry his products exclusive of his competition for the first year.

If you've selected a location, take him to see it. Provide him with as much information about your plan as he'll listen to. Ask him if he has other ideas as to how you can make this a mutually profitable deal.

After you have finished your pitch, make sure you *close*. Ask him if he is prepared to supply you. If the answer is no, call his boss. What do you have to lose? The salesperson may not like that you've gone above him, but if you don't get the line, that sales rep can't hurt you.

If you strike out with the sales manager, and the line is important enough, go to the president. Many company owners are more aggressive about opening new accounts than the sales force. (Maybe the sales force is on straight salary, and they just see your account as extra work. Possibly the salesperson has a favorite buddy close to your proposed location whom he is trying to protect.)

After you've exhausted every avenue, put this matter in the tickler file for later. If the line is important enough, you'll want to try again in six months or a year.

How many vendors will you need? Is it possible to have too many? You need to have as many suppliers as necessary to provide you with the full range of goods and services you need to do business and to have adequate backup for those hard-to-get resources. You may also want to have competitive suppliers on a number of items that are commonly available to make certain you're getting the right price.

It's definitely possible to have too many vendors. Each vendor represents a cost to your purchasing and bookkeeping departments. In other words, for each supplier, there will be a sales rep calling who'll take up the time of the person in charge of buying that line. This has a cost equal to the lost opportunity of what that person could have been doing to add sales or profit if she had not been with the salesperson. Also, each supplier will be sending you invoices. Each invoice must be posted and eventually paid. This will cost you bookkeeping time and the cost of checks, envelopes, and stamps. To the extent that you are slow paying, or there is a disagreement about your account, there will be additional time spent working these things out.

In business today, there's a great emphasis on reducing the number of suppliers, and I would agree that a business should be wary. However, I would argue that it's better to have too many than too few. It's very hard to sell out of an empty store.

At this point in your business plan, you will want to list your primary suppliers and provide a short paragraph on each as to their benefit to your business.

Part 4 The Physical Plant

We've already discussed the selection of your business location. A related but distinct issue is determining the size and layout requirements of the facility.

For many enterprises, this should also be a multipart

plan. To illustrate this, let me use as an example a typical wholesale distributor.

Blake is a supplier of small parts such as electronic devices. His new business will supply these to retailers in a city of three million. Later he hopes to expand to the whole state and beyond.

Depending on size, it's not impossible for Blake to set up operations in a garage. A step up from that would be a mini-storage warehouse. Because the parts are small, he should be able to warehouse quite an inventory in a very small facility. An additional advantage to such a first location is that he can rent month to month and not commit to a long-term lease.

Blake may want to include in his business plan this type of warehouse along with the rent and terms. He might then predict a sales level at which it will be necessary and affordable to move into a larger unit. Possibly the second location would include four hundred square feet of reception and office space, and four thousand square feet of warehouse with a loading dock.

He may expect that he'll occupy that facility for three years until sales reach $1 million, at which time he'll move to a ten-thousand-square-foot building. Blake's intentions might even include purchasing this unit.

Whether or not you go into this kind of detail about your future plans, you do need to produce a list of "needs" for your first facility. You may also want to create a "want" list. Do you need a loading dock? Do you need a sprinkler system because of the type of inventory you will carry? Do you need carpeted floors? Two bathrooms? Lots of window display space? Two-twenty electrical service? High ceilings?

How much space do you really need? It's very easy to put yourself in a situation where you're in business to pay the landlord. Unless you have unlimited funds, you'll do well to start off with the minimum amount of space possible. Then be willing to move a time or two if your sales goals are met.

There are times when this advice won't apply. If you'll have a large investment in fixed equipment such as in a restaurant or a manufacturing plant, you may have to take a risk on a larger space. The cost of moving these types of enterprises dictates moving less than might be the case for a retailer, wholesaler, or service provider. (How much can it cost to move a tax preparation office?)

Golden nugget: *Don't burden your new business with more overhead than it needs in space rental.* Start small and build as necessary.

Add to your business plan as much detail as you think is necessary concerning your physical plant, along with any up-front costs necessary to implement your plan.

Part 5 The Advertising Plan

Your business plan should include how you intend to approach the complicated issue of advertising. The issues that should be addressed include:

1.   How much will you budget for advertising the first year?

2.   What basis will you use for determining your budget in the second and ensuing years?

3.   Whom do you expect to reach with your message?

4.   What advertising media will you use to reach your audience?

5.   What message do you expect to convey to your campaign?

It's the rare business that can build beyond a meagre beginning without advertising. At the very least, almost every businesses should have a presence on the Web. At the other end of the spectrum, entertainment firms such as nightclubs or movie theatres have to spend a good portion of their start-up money getting out the word that they're in town.

If your business depends on the Internet, you may wish to plan your opening around the timing that your website will be complete. You might also try to start establishing yourself on GoogleMyBusiness even before you open.

In determining your advertising strategy, begin by writing down again, in detail, who your customers are. Are you selling to consumers, dealers, OEMs, the government? Are you selling in a five-zip code area, citywide, across a five-state region, internationally? Are your customers a certain age and sex, or do they fit into some other special group?

It's important to realize that you may have more than one type of customer who needs to be reached by your message. Take the case of a manufacturer, for instance.

A manufacturer may be selling to a wholesaler, who in turn sells to retailers. The retailer finally sells the same product to a consumer. The manufacturer ends up having at least five customers to whom it will be advantageous to deliver information about the product.

He must sell the buyer at the wholesale level. If the wholesale buyer isn't convinced about the need for your product, the retailer and consumer will never have a chance to make a decision. At this level, it may also be important that the buyer's supervisor and/or the owner of the company is also knowledgeable about your product and feels confident it can be sold.

Next in the chain is the salesperson who represents the wholesaler. If she doesn't take the time to show your item or is not convincing when she shows it to the dealer, you may find your product bottlenecked at the wholesale level.

The wholesale sales rep's job will be made easier if the owner or buyer at the dealer level is already aware of the product when she walks in. Thus you may wish to advertise to this level also.

It does little good to persuade the retailer to purchase your item if his salesclerks don't know why the consumer would ever want one. This clerk represents the fourth link in the chain.

Finally, if the consumer visits a retailer and is already primed to buy, you can create some real excitement that may be translated all the way back up the distribution chain. If the dealer sells out quickly, you can be certain that he'll reorder. If he reorders, the salesperson will spread the word to his other customers as well as to his fellow sales clerks. If the wholesaler quickly empties his shelf, he may place a larger second order.

A manufacturer might have the resources to reach all five of these levels at once. Unfortunately, it would break the company's back. As a result, each year they must decide which of these levels is the most important to attack.

One year a company might spend most of their ad dollars on trade magazine advertising. These ads are designed to reach the wholesale buyer, his salesperson, the dealer, and his clerk. However, if we want to be certain to reach the wholesale buyer with a message that is not appropriate for the dealer, it might be better to use email or even snail mail.

Another year they might allocate most of the ad budget to consumer magazine and Internet advertising. The dealer and wholesale personnel also read these special-interest magazines. However, if they are specifically trying to reach the consumer, the answer could be in-store merchandisers such as brochures or displays.

Write into your business plan a list of "customers" to whom you need to communicate your message.

The following is a list of media that are available, with a short paragraph about each. The Appendix will suggest some further reading that can provide more depth.

The Web. Today, a Web presence is generally the most important advertising avenue for any business. And the good news is that you can get a lot of bang for a very few bucks. A rudimentary Web page can be constructed by any fifteen-year-old. Such a website will give your customers a place to see your story and pictures, descriptions, and prices of your basic product or service lines. And your own Web address can cost as little as $100 per year. Providers like Wix.com are very easy to use. There is a special website development article in our online materials. Go to https://WhenFridayIsntPayday.com and find page 110

Your Web page is so important that for many businesses, it exists before the business opens. You can test the water and see how many hits you get, even before you have a location or phone number.

In addition to your own site, there are many ways to advertise on the Web. Industry associations often have sites where you can be listed for free. Other for-profit organizations might offer some free listings in hopes of getting you to pay for upgrades and placement. Paying for placement in search engines or paying services to help you get better exposure on search engines are other avenues of using the Web.

E-mail. We all hate Spam! Or do we? I've heard business owners say: "I'm not going to send out emails, because I hate to get them. Golden Nugget: ***Don't ever project your opinions on to the general public.***

Your emails shouldn't be Spam. You should have permission to send these ads and offer an opt-out for those who've had enough. In this author's opinion e-mail has had the greatest impact on business efficiency of any invention in fifty years. It is a fast and cheap method to communicate with your customers, vendors, sales force, and even the bank.

You will almost certainly want to create your own e-mail database of customers willing to receive updates, sales, or new product information from your company. In addition, there is very likely one or more services in your industry that will e-mail your information to their database of opted-in companies or individuals.

Trade magazines. Almost every trade has specialized magazines (often online), newsletters, and/or buying guides that are distributed to members of the trade at very little or no cost. The cost of advertising in these publications is usually very low. Do some research into how well read the trade publications in your industry are. One may be quite popular, while another may go right into the trash.

Specialty magazines. These range from slick four-color magazines to four-page newsprint club papers. Often, use of them will enable you to reach the consumer of your product or service more efficiently. For instance, if you're selling professional ice skates, you'll be better off advertising in a magazine read by amateur and professional ice skaters as opposed to, say, *Sports Illustrated,* which is marketed to a more general audience. There is a wide range of pricing for this type of magazine, depending upon the circulation and quality of the publication.

General interest magazines. You will want to consider such magazines as *People, Business Week, Inc,* and so on only if you have a product that appeals to the majority of the public, and if you have a national distribution network. It's rare indeed that the owner of a business with fewer than ten employees will want to risk the cost of an ad in these publications. The cost of a single page can be tens of thousands of dollars.

General circulation newspapers. Local or regional retailers and service providers may do very well advertising in newspapers that serve their customers. Newspaper advertising is fairly expensive, however. Additionally, you, the advertiser, are competing for the reader's attention with a lot of other advertising. In general, the newspaper is useless for younger customers, and almost useless entirely.

Outdoor advertising. Billboards, bus benches, and other outdoor media are a much-overlooked method of getting exposure. It's possible to get into this in a big way or a small way. One friend of mine took only a single ad on one bus bench near his retail store with excellent results. Many restaurants off the main drag use a billboard on the main drag to direct potential diners to their location.

A variation of outdoor advertising would be your own signs and window displays. If you expect to attract traffic because of your store's location, buy the biggest, boldest sign you can afford (and the law will allow). If you have a window display, spend time and effort making it attractive and *interesting*. Don't be afraid to make your window display a bit weird. You want to attract attention! Otherwise, why spend the extra money on that great location?

Mailings. Among the least expensive ways (even in the days of ever-increasing postal rates) of reaching your specific customer with a very specific message is the mail. You can buy lists of prospects broken out by almost any criterion you can imagine. It may seem far-fetched, but you should be able to buy a list of all the single folks between the ages of twenty and forty, with above-average incomes, in the five closest zip codes to your business. Look for sellers of such lists online under "Mailing Lists."

You may also be able to reach your customer through a "stack" mailing. I'm certain you've seen the little stacks of postcards that come to you in a plastic-wrapped package. It costs you only a few cents each to participate in that kind of mailing program. Check with the trade and consumer magazines in your industry for help in locating companies that do this type of mailing. Check for listings with Standard Rate and Data. Larger libraries should have a copy or you can search online.

There are companies that are in the specific business of doing mailings for other businesses. They can help you design your piece; sell you a list; and print, fold, address, and mail the item on their bulk-rate permit. Again, you should be able to find help for this on the Internet under "Mailing Services."

EDDM or Every Door Direct Mail is the best way to reach consumers or businesses if you want to saturate specific neighborhoods. In this case, you are sending out a bulk postcard with no address. The card is delivered to every household, every business, or both on specific carrier routes. You supply the exact quantity needed. There are printers who will do all the work for you, including helping design the card. Look up EDDM on the Web.

If you are a manufacturer or wholesaler or otherwise deal on a regional or national level, there is usually a list supplier that specializes in your industry. Check with your association or an industry buyer's guide.

Radio. Unlike the local newspaper, radio still offers a way to get your message to a broad spectrum of people in your territory. And you can get great bang for your buck in the less-sought-after time periods. The salesperson for the radio station is often an accomplished copywriter who may be able to help you write your ad for free.

Television. Cable television has created an opportunity for even the smallest business to take advantage of the advertising power of TV. There are packagers who'll provide you with everything from the script to airtime purchases for a set fee. You may find TV to be especially appropriate for your grand opening or other special sales situations. Contact your local cable television station for suggestions as to suppliers of these services.

Trade shows. Most manufacturers and distributors aren't considered to be "in the business" if they aren't attending some of the special trade shows offered by their industry. My own experience has shown that it's possible to give the impression that you're much bigger than you really are by taking a large space and doing a good decorating job.

Consumer shows. Local businesses that serve consumers also have opportunities for shows. These may be special-interest shows like a home show or boat show. They might also be more general exhibitions put on by the local chamber of commerce, or as part of a county fair.

You might also be able to put together your own exhibit at a local mall. You may not be able to afford a shop in the mall full-time, but you may be able to take a kiosk during a peak season for your type of product.

Public relations. Frequently referred to as free advertising, PR can be many times more effective than paid advertising. If you can come up with a special-interest story about your business that the media will latch on to, it can provide a dose of credibility. People believe editorial ink more than they believe advertising.

Publicity stories are usually easier to place in trade publications. Most will publish a short release about a new product, change in location, or appointment of a new salesperson. Use this venue as much as possible. It isn't absolutely free since it takes time to write a release and a few dollars for photos, but it's far more cost efficient than paid advertising.

Premiums. Pens, calendars, notebooks, clocks, and many other products can attractively display your name or logo, and at the same time make an attractive gift for you to give to your customer. Premiums such as these represent a low-cost, but potentially very effective, way to get your message to a specific group of customers.

With this range of possible advertising venues in mind, you'll now want to begin to decide what approach to take to get your message out. Part of that process will include whether or not to use an advertising agency.

Unless you've had substantial advertising experience, have access to someone who does, or likes to burn up your money with no idea of whether or not it will bring results, you'll need the help of a professional advertising agency. Even in the best of situations advertising is not an exact science. You can hire the best, follow their directions exactly, and still not get the results you hoped for. However, well-planned and executed advertising can produce remarkable results.

When you're starting out and don't have much money for advertising, it's difficult to attract a large, well-established agency. Using the recommendations of others, the Internet, or chamber of commerce, you'll want to look at the qualifications and portfolios of several agencies before making your selection. If nothing else, these interviews will teach you a great deal about how advertising works.

There are two kinds of agencies. Most of the larger ones are full-service, meaning that they can handle every aspect of the campaign from concept to paste-up and placement. Smaller agencies, by contrast, specialize in one or another portion of the business. In the early stages of your development, you'll want an agency that is versatile enough to make an intelligent suggestion as to the best media for you to use. Once you've decided how much money to allocate to each category, you should ask the agency's account executive some serious questions about the agency's ability to develop the actual ad.

For instance, a good agency will tell you if you need to spend 25 percent of your budget on outdoor advertising, even if it hasn't had experience in this area. Then it will help you find someone who does.

With respect to advertising, you should set specific goals that you want to achieve. Maybe over the course of a six-week campaign you want to increase the number of people walking through your door by 35 percent. Possibly you want 30 percent of the people in your market to be able to identify you and your product within one year. Fifty new clients with opening orders of five hundred dollars or more within six months might make you happy.

Tell the advertising agency what your goal is. They should honestly tell you whether they believe advertising can achieve that goal. If you fall substantially short of your plan and assuming you have not interfered with the agency's suggested approach, it is very likely the fault of the agency. Consider a new one.

At this point in your business plan, you'll want to describe the advertising plan that you have for your opening. Possibly you'll want to include some rough sketches of the concept. Indicate the budget, the media, the frequency, and, above all, the goal.

Next, include a statement of the method you'll use to appropriate advertising money for future budgets. Possible approaches might include a percentage of last year's sales, a percentage of projected sales, a dollar amount that seems affordable.

It's important to remember one major limitation of advertising. The best campaign in the world will get the customer to try your product, service, or store only once. Ultimately, what keeps the customer coming back is quality and service.

Please find more on small specialized agencies and much more on marketing at **https://WhenFridayIsntPayday.com** Look for page 116

Part 6 Projecting Your Income

Before getting into the meat of this section, I'd like to drive home two points:

1.   Do *not* plan to lose money your first year. Do not even plan to lose money in your first month. I can't tell you how many ill-conceived business plans have been created that offer investors nothing but losses for the first year or three.

2.   Do *not* plan to work for *free* for the first year. If you don't take a salary for your efforts, you're kidding yourself about the success of your enterprise. If you currently make $40,000 per year and your business breaks even in its first year with you taking no salary, the company has really lost $40,000. If you take $50,000 a year after that, you will only be back to even at the end of five years.

Charge your company a reasonable amount for your services. It's not unreasonable to take a small cut from your previous salary, but don't work cheap or for free. In section 1 I showed you a budget that I felt you'd understand since it was similar to a household budget. The budget that you'll now be shown is a more appropriate way to evaluate and plan a business. It's called a profit-and-loss statement, or an income statement.

Business is based on percentages. Using the family budget

approach, you have no analytical tools. That method is commonly referred to as "running your business out of the check book": If there is money in the bank, everything is okay. If you don't have money in the bank, you must be doing something wrong. Even if that were true (which it isn't) this simplistic method wouldn't tell you where to make changes. To put money in the bank, you would be just as likely to cut highly productive employees as you would to considering a price increase.

The percentage method helps you to determine whether a layoff or a price hike is likely to produce the optimum result. Using the income statement method that follows, it's possible to analyze each aspect of your business to determine where you need to make adjustments.

DEFINING THE TERMS

Gross sales. The total amount of income generated from all sales activities. This would include such things as sales of merchandise, services, meals, buildings, rentals, or commissions. It's restricted to those items that represent your regular business activity. It would not include, for instance, income from the rental of extra space in your facility, or interest income on a savings account.

Cost of goods sold (or services delivered). The total cost you have paid to make the goods or services in your gross sales ready for sale. The cost of raw material, labor, machine time, and overhead would be an example of the costs of goods sold for a manufacturer. If the product wasn't ready for sale until it was packaged, then it would be necessary to add the cost of packaging materials, labor, and associated overhead to complete the packaging.

In a service business, most of the costs are labor and overhead. There's an important difference between the two. A dental assistant, for example, is part of the cost of services, not the general overhead.

Gross profit. When the cost of goods is subtracted from the gross sales, what is left is the gross profit. If you buy ten apples for $1 apiece (cost of goods = $10), and sell all ten for $3 each (gross sales = $30), you are left with a gross profit of $20 ($30 - $10 = $20).

Overhead. Those items that are required to support the activities of the business, but not necessary to the production of the product or service. Bookkeeping, office expenses, administrative payroll, commissions, royalties, advertising, and other such expenses fall into the category of overhead.

Fixed overhead. Those portions of the total overhead that tend to remain the same regardless of total sales. Rent, office payroll, phone, depreciation of office equipment and furniture, postage, and office supplies are some of the items that represent the fixed overhead.

Variable overhead. Expenses that are more generally seen as a percentage of sales or that can be quickly adjusted to varying sales conditions. Sales commissions, royalties, and product liability insurance are examples of the cost of doing business that is generally seen as a percentage of sales. Advertising, promotions, research and development, and travel might be viewed as expenses that can be quickly cut or expanded, depending on specific circumstances.

Net profit. The result of subtracting all overhead, both fixed and variable from gross profits. (Also known as the "bottom line.") In our apple cart example above, you may have paid two dollars to rent the cart for the day, and a 10 percent commission to the salesperson. Thus you would have had a total overhead of five dollars (two dollars in fixed overhead and three dollars in a variable). This would leave you with a ten-dollar profit for the day (fifteen dollars gross profit minus five dollars in total overhead).

The following formula should be memorized, dissected, and thoroughly understood before you open your doors:

Gross Sales
Cost of Goods (or Services)
Gross Profit
Overhead = Net Profit

Here is the income statement of a very basic retail operation.

Gross sales	$1,500	100%
Cost of goods	900	60
Gross profit	600	40
Overhead		
Variable		
Advertising	75	5
Commission	45	3
Fixed		
Rent	150	10
Salary	90	6
Phone	60	4
Postage	30	2
Total overhead	450	30
Net profit	$ 150	10%

Each item is shown as a dollar amount. Then the amount is restated as a percentage of gross sales (e.g., salary is 6 percent of gross sales).

As sales increase or decrease, it's possible to see how some of these line items change relative to one another by watching the percentages change. In the following example, we see what might happen if sales doubled.

Gross sales	$3,000	100%
Cost of sales	1,800	60
Gross profit	1,200	40
Overhead		
Variable		
Advertising	150	5
Commission	90	3
Fixed		
Rent	150	5
Salary	90	3
Phone	60	2
Postage	30	1
Total overhead	570	19
Net profit	$ 630	21%

Overhead increased a few dollars but dropped dramatically in the percentage of gross sales. This resulted in a substantial increase in profit.

Most businesses are far more complex than the above example. Let's revisit each of the basic definitions covered thus far in part 6, and add a little meat to those bare bones.

Gross sales. Sometimes referred to as gross revenues to provide a broader-based classification, this is the total dollars received in any given period (day, week, month, year) from any source. In an uncomplicated business, this might represent all the receipts from the sale of products or services. In some businesses, there may be income from both sales of products and delivery of services. Examples would be a locksmith who sells locks and also repairs them; an optometrist who examines your eyes, but also sells glasses and contact lenses; or an appliance store that sells you a stove and offers installation at a charge.

In these instances, it may make sense to break out the sales from products on one line and the revenue from services on a separate line.

A portion of your revenue might not really belong to you. For instance, if you must charge sales tax, you are merely holding the money for the government. This amount must be subtracted from gross sales.

Other amounts are commonly subtracted from this first figure. Discounts, returns, sales taxes, and other credits are usually shown on the second line since these are amounts that reduce your gross revenue.

Cost of goods sold or services delivered. This line can become quite complicated. Accounting and tax rules are forever changing concerning what is and what is not a cost of goods. In general, this amount is how much you paid for the goods that you sold in this period.

If you didn't carry inventory from period to period this would be easy to figure. If you purchased $550 in product on day one of the periods and sold all of it before the end of the period for $1,000, it wouldn't take a computer for you to know your cost was $550 and gross profit was $450. Life is not so simple, however. Let's say that you have $120 worth of inventory at cost left at the end of the period. Now your cost of goods was $550 minus $120, or $430. Your sales were still $1,000, so your gross profit is now $570.

In the real world, you also started with inventory. Continuing with the same example, let's say you had $75 worth of inventory at the beginning. Now your cost of goods would be: beginning inventory plus purchases minus ending inventory, or $75 + $550 - $120 = $505. There is still no change in your sales, so $ 1,000 - $505 = $495, which is now your gross profit.

Other things affecting cost of goods include freight-in (cost of shipping product from supplier to you), labor to prepare the item for sale, and any other charges directly related to the sale of the item. A very complicated gross profit analysis for products might look like this:

Gross Sales	$11,000	100.0%
Less Discount	800	7.3
Returns	300	2.7
Adjusted Gross Sales	9,900	90.0
Cost of Goods		
Beginning Inventory	$ 2,400	
Plus: Purchases $6,100		
Freight-in 500		
Direct Labor 2,350		
Less: End Inventory -6,800		
Cost of goods sold	$ 4,600	41.8
Gross Profit	$ 5,300	48.2%

Later, you'll see that if you are losing money, an increase of 5 percent in your sales price will result in $550 more gross profit and a gross profit percentage of 53.2 percent. That assumes that you still sell as many units. You could achieve the same result by buying the product for about 9 percent less or reducing the labor cost necessary to make it salable by $550. You could also do a little of each. Thus you can begin to see how this system allows you to make management decisions.

Please note: All the above references are only to those items that you purchase and inventory for resale. When you buy a workbench or a computer, it is not included in "purchases" or in inventory.

Gross profit. What kind of gross profit percentage do you need for your business? The answer may be as low as 5 percent or as high as 70 percent depending on the kind of business you are in. Here are a few examples:

Retail hardware store	33-40%
Italian restaurant	66%
Manufacturer of consumer goods	50%
Auto retailer	10%
Parts wholesaler	28%

For more information about the appropriate profit margin for your industry, call the trade association or the editor of one of the trade magazines. In many industries, there may even be statistics available on what others are doing. Almost every industry has this information online.

PROFIT ANALYSIS FOR A SERVICE BUSINESS

How should you use this approach if you are in a service business? In the simplest example, you are the sole service provider. Figure out how many hours per month you spend actually providing that service or in direct preparation for doing so.

For instance, you are an auto mechanic. You work seventy hours per week. Out of this, however, you spend twenty hours in administrative tasks having nothing to do with servicing cars. You do count, however, the time you spend calling or driving around for parts, cleaning up, and explaining the bill to the customer.

You conclude that you are spending fifty hours providing services. You are paying yourself $700 per week, for a total of seventy hours of work. An easy calculation shows you are earning $10 per hour. Fifty hours at $10 per hour means that your cost of service is $500. Your cost-of-service analysis would look like this.

Gross sales	$1,500	100.0%	
Cost of services	500	33.3	_____
Gross profit	$1,000	66.7%	

Again, this can become more complicated by taking into account discounts and items directly related to the delivery of the service. In the case of the auto mechanic, the cost of service could include rags, lubricating greases, or other items not billed specifically to the customer.

PROFIT ANALYSIS FOR A COMPLEX BUSINESS

If you're selling two or more very different kinds of products that result in dramatically different margins for each, you may wish to separate them on your statement. This is also true if you offer dramatically different types of services or a combination of product sales and services.

For instance, one of my companies had six different profit centers that were separately shown in the gross-profit analysis. Each one was evaluated according to its own purchases, freight factors, inventory changes, labor factors, and service components. By breaking the company into these six parts we were able to evaluate each on its own merits, rather than guessing that each is carrying its own weight. If any part is not contributing to profits, we were able to make appropriate adjustments specific to that portion of the business.

General and administrative overhead. The costs of doing business that is not directly related to the cost of goods fall under the category of general and administrative overhead. Under this category, place everything from telephones and rent to office salaries and payroll taxes. Those items that do not necessarily increase or decrease as sales go up or down will be shown in the budget as a dollar amount. Those items that generally fluctuate in accordance with sales will be shown as a percentage.

For instance, generally, rent, casualty insurance, and trash service will be the same month after month. Thus you would put these items in at their dollar amount.

Salaries, telephone, depreciation, and other similar categories may change from month to month and might even increase or decrease in a pattern similar to sales. However, in most cases, it is harder to predict these amounts by using a percentage of sales than if you project a dollar amount.

Line items that are commonly shown as a percentage would be commissions, royalties, utilities (for a manufacturer), product liability insurance, freight out for those giving freight allowance, phone expense for phone sales operations, and advertising.

Your statement for general and administrative expenses might look something like this (assuming $20,000 in sales):

GENERAL AND ADMINISTRATIVE EXPENSES

Office salaries		$3,300	16.50%
Payroll taxes		330	1.65
Rent		1,250	6.25
Utilities		350	1.75
Interest		550	2.75
Travel		200	1.00
Office supplies		200	1.00
Depreciation		600	3.00
Commissions	6%	1,200	
Freight-out	1%	200	
Advertising	5%	1,000	
Insurance	1%	200	
Total general and Administrative expenses		$9,380	46.90%

If your sales of $20,000 in this example had generated a gross profit of $10,000, you would now subtract the general and administrative expenses from the gross profit ($10,000 - $9,380) and you would arrive at the profit for that period of $620.

Finally, you would want to include an amount for income tax. This is shown after the net profit and is subtracted from net profit to produce the final line on your budget: "Net profit after tax."

For most individuals, the first projected income statement they will want to construct will be their ideal budget. It will project sales as realistically as possible given the prospective owner's knowledge. The cost of goods and gross profit will reflect information supplied by the trade or from the owner's personal knowledge.

The other expenses will be shown at the highest amount within a range of expectations.

Let's take a minute to make that last paragraph concrete. You are going to open a retail auto-parts store. You can imagine in your dreams or nightmares that the monthly sales might range from $100 to $100,000 in the first twelve months. You've talked to owners of similar businesses, the local trade association, and the sales representatives from three prospective suppliers. From these, you would narrow the realistic sales number to a range of $ 10,000 to $60,000, but the consensus seems to be in the range of $20,000. If you want to be very conservative in your approach, you might even use $15,000.

Further investigation shows the cost of goods sold averages about 66 percent, leaving a gross profit of 34 percent. You might figure that your cost of goods could be a little higher in the early going in that you may not buy as well as an experienced dealer. You may also find yourself discounting to your customers in the early going to keep from losing a marginal sale. Thus you may want to figure your cost of goods at 70 percent.

If you already have a location, you know the rent. If not, you will have to make your best guess. If you are certain that you will employ one clerk at $1,000 per month and you will pay yourself $800, you can show an exact figure there. Most companies will figure payroll taxes at around 10 percent of payroll. Now you have that figure. Earlier you were supposed to arrive at a formula for advertising. Put that one in.

Continue the process until you have what will represent your best guess as to what the company will actually do in each category. This becomes your working budget, the one to which you will compare each month's actual figures.

Part 7 The Break-Even Analysis

The break-even analysis takes the information that you have compiled in your income statement and looks at it backward. Given your best guess at the costs of doing business, this analysis asks the question: If these are my actual costs, what volume of sales must I do to break even (no profit and no loss)?

For this example, we'll assume a company that has figured their dollar amount of general and administrative overhead (sometimes referred to as fixed expenses) to be $1,000 per month. Their percentage amount (also known as variable expenses) of general and administrative overhead is 15 percent of gross sales. Their cost of goods is 40 percent.

Our question now becomes a formula that might look something like this:

Gross sales	$X	100%
- Cost of Goods	-.40X	-40
Gross Profit	$.60X	60%
- variable expense	-.15X	-15%
- fixed expense	-$900	-45
	$0	0%

Note that fixed expense had to be 45 percent for net profit to be 0 percent.

We now have one line (in bold letters) that shows the relationship between the percentage amounts and the dollar amount. $900 = 45 percent. Thus we can create the equation $X/$900 = 100%/45%. After employing some freshman algebra we arrive at the formula X = 90,000/45 or X = $2,000. Thus you have determined that this business would have to produce $2,000 in gross sales during this period to break even. We would also be able to determine that if the fixed expenses stay fixed, this owner can expect to make a profit equal to 45 percent of every additional dollar he sells.

To arrive at your break-even without going through all the algebra, remember to divide fixed expenses in dollars by fixed expenses in percentage. The result will be the gross volume of sales needed to break even.

At this point produce for your business plan a projection of income statements for the first year by month. Also, produce a break-even analysis. You may also want to produce income statements for years two and three if you expect more than 10 percent growth in each year.

You will find substantial additional information online at **https://WhenFridayIsntPayday.com** Look for page 128. Included is a section on using financial statements to dramatically improve the overall performance of your company. Another article will delve into various pricing methods.

CHAPTER

3

Legal Requirements

Part 1 Enterprise Type

You'll need to decide before opening the business what form your business will take. As mentioned in chapter 3 of section 1, in the United States there are four approaches available. In other countries it will be necessary to check with local resources to determine the choices offered.

Sole proprietorship. Most very small businesses use this enterprise type. It is the simplest from a tax and legal standpoint. In many cases, part-time businesses using the sole proprietor approach will not even segregate their personal financial affairs from their business income and expenses. While this is not the best way to run any company, it is possible.

In general, the steps for establishing a sole proprietorship include:

A.   Determination of a name. If you're not going to use your own name as the business name, you must file a "fictitious business statement or DBA." The government requires this filing so as to put your vendors and customers on notice that you are the responsible   party   behind   the   "fictitious   name."

In most jurisdictions, this filing is accomplished by publishing certain information three times in a general circulation newspaper. If you will open your daily paper to the beginning of the want ads you will see a section titled something like "legal notices." Most papers publish new fictitious business statements every day. You will generally also need to file with a local or state authority. Search the Internet for How to file a DBA and your state. If you decide to use your own name, it's not necessary to file this statement. For instance, a professional firm named John Doe and Associates would not need to file. However, John's Baby Furniture would. If you're not certain, it's better to file.

B.   Next, you should open a checking account in the company name. The bank will require a copy of your fictitious business filing before they'll open the account. It is not absolutely necessary to have a separate checking account, but it's highly recommended.

C.   If you will have employees, you should apply for a federal ID number. You can use your Social Security number in a sole proprietorship, but it doesn't cost anything to get a special number for your business.

D.   In most states, you'll need a sales tax number. This is the way that the state identifies you for the purposes of collecting sales taxes from you, your customers, and your vendors. You'll need this number regardless of the type of business you'll be running or the enterprise form you select. Your vendors will require this number in order to sell you items tax-free that you intend to resell.

Generally, the state will ask for a cash deposit to ensure your payment of future sales taxes. If you sell only to other businesses who have sales tax numbers, you won't have any tax liability, and thus—in most states—you shouldn't have to make a deposit.

However, if you'll be selling to consumers, end users, or others who must pay a sales tax for the products or services you provide, then you'll certainly be asked for a deposit.

Most entrepreneurs are optimistic and somewhat proud of their enterprise. As a result, when the clerk at the sales tax office asks you to provide an estimate of your first quarter's or year's income, there is a tendency to give a high figure. The amount you state will be used to determine the amount of your deposit. In other words, the more optimistic you are, the more out-of-pocket expense you'll have.

A better approach is to come up with the lowest estimate that you think will be believed. If the clerk doesn't agree with your number and attempts to have you increase it, there's no rule against continuing to argue your position. If the difference of opinion is great enough, you may even want to involve a supervisor. The clerk's job is to get the largest deposit possible. Your job is to pay the smallest amount possible.

Please understand. This in no way affects your future tax liability, only your immediate cash flow. And remember, this general rule of not overestimating your income applies to *all* deposits you might make.

The positive aspect of the sole proprietorship as an enterprise type is that it is uncomplicated and inexpensive. The negative is that you have unlimited personal liability for the debts or other liabilities that may arise in running the business. You have less flexibility in your tax matters. In addition, you may find it more difficult to raise capital. Addressing these issues one at a time, the most important by far is the matter of unlimited personal liability.

You may or may not currently own a home, substantial savings, stocks, bonds, or other commercial paper. If you don't now, you certainly intend to build such assets in the future. You may even intend to own a vacation home, boat, jewelry, or art. As a sole proprietor, everything you own is subject to being seized by your business creditors.

Here are two examples of what can happen. Let's say that you currently own your own home, which is worth $150,000, and it has a mortgage of $70,000. You also have stocks and other holdings worth $25,000. You intend to open the business with your savings of $20,000. After six months in business, you decide to close down due to continuous losses. You are out of cash and owe suppliers $40,000. You signed a lease that has eighteen months to go at $500 per month. You also failed to pay employee tax deposits of $10,000.

Your vendors, the landlord, and the government will go after your home, stock, and anything else that isn't nailed down to collect the $59,000 you owe. And they will have every legal right.

In case number two, you go into the business with every penny you can scrape together. You live in an apartment and drive an old, beat-up VW. Five years later you are very successful. You have net assets worth $500,000 in addition to the book value (assets minus liabilities) of the business. One of your customers has an accident using one of your products. The manufacturer is out of business. You are the retailer. The customer successfully sues your business for $2 million. Your insurance pays the first million. Your business is able to come up with another $250,000. Your customer may next go after every asset you own personally.

This liability exposure is true for sole proprietorships, partnerships, and the general partners in a limited partnership. Only through incorporation can you escape this potential disaster.

Regarding the tax flexibility issue, 100 percent of the income of the business is taxed at the rate applicable to the owner as an individual. Under tax law in 2018, there is a slight disadvantage compared to regular corporation taxation. Of course, the government is always changing the rules, so consult your attorney or CPA to determine the current situation.

The real problem for the sole proprietor is the lack of flexibility. The owner of a corporation will have an easier time writing off certain expenses that may be perceived as personal or partly personal in a corporate tax return than will her counterpart in a sole proprietorship. In the second instance the small business return is part of the owner's tax return. With a corporation, it is an entirely different filing. We don't mention these issues of scrutiny with any intention of suggesting illegal tax avoidance. The point is, in a sole proprietorship situation even appropriate write-offs will get a tougher look in the owner's personal tax return.

A sole proprietor also has fewer options for pension, profit sharing, and employee benefit programs. Many of these have substantial tax advantages, but are available only to corporations.

Additionally, you may not be able to raise funds as easily with a sole proprietorship. Banks and other financial institutions who lend to companies prefer that the owner's liability be limited to the net worth of the business, as in a corporation. Why? Because, unless the corporation is rock solid, the bank will also ask for a personal guarantee from the owners. Then it will be the only entity that can attempt to take your personal assets if your company fails. In the case of a sole proprietorship, *all* creditors would have access to the owner's personal assets.

You are also limited in raising funds from others. The only method available is loans. Only through the other enterprise types can you raise money by offering ownership.

Partnerships. A partnership is identical in every aspect to a sole proprietorship except that everything is split among the partners. Thus, the personal liability will now extend to any partner. Creditors or individuals with judgments against the company can now attempt to get satisfaction by attaching any or all the partners' assets.

The partnership does file a separate tax return, which helps to make expenses easier to claim. However, the same tax-advantaged programs (pensions, profit sharing, and so forth) that are unavailable to the sole proprietor are also unavailable to partnerships.

When it comes to raising money, the partnership has an advantage in that banks now have potentially greater assets to use as collateral to secure loans. They will ask for personal guarantees from each partner. In addition, partnerships are often used as a method to raise capital by adding owners. If your partnership now has two individuals owning 50 percent each, it may be possible to entice a third partner to bring extra money into the business by giving up part of that ownership. For instance, you may need fifty thousand dollars. A potential investor who likes your business says he is willing to put in the funds for 40 percent of the business. This would leave you and your original partner with 30 percent each. It is possible to do this as often as you like. There is no limit to the number of partners in a partnership.

Limited partnerships. This form is much like a regular partnership except that only the "general partners" have unlimited liability. The "limited partners" (investors) have their liability limited to the amount of their investment. The determination of who is a general and who is a limited partner is decided solely by the partners. And generally, limited partners are not actively involved with the day-to-day running of the business.

Corporations. The second most popular form of enterprise is the corporation. It provides the ultimate protection from personal liability and the maximum amount of flexibility. In addition, the small corporation may be the least scrutinized form of business by government or tax authorities. The corporation generally has a wider range of ways to raise funds. Finally, the corporation enjoys the widest range of opportunities for special tax benefits.

A corporation is owned by its stockholders. There may be one stockholder holding all the shares, or there may be millions of shareholders holding various amounts of shares. Without going into details that are far beyond the scope of a business this size, I should point out that it is also possible for corporations to sell various classes of shares with various rights and preferences. For the very small business, we can limit our discussion to three types of simple corporations: the regular, or "C" corporation, which is taxed directly by the IRS; the "Sub S" corporation, where the earnings are passed through to the stockholders, who must pay the tax personally; and the LLC, which is similar to a "S", but yet very different.

All three of these forms limit the financial exposure of the owners to their actual investment and any value in the corporation beyond that investment. This is the single greatest advantage of a corporation. However, the shareholders can lose this protection if they don't completely separate the affairs of the corporation from their own personal affairs. They must also be certain that the amount of the original investment is clearly adequate to protect the public and the vendors from the likely activities of the corporation.

Let's examine these three concepts in reverse order. When a state grants one or more individuals the privilege of opening a corporation, it is only willing to shield the individual owners from personal liability in return for an expectation that the corporation will be able to adequately cover that exposure by itself.

Take, for instance, a company with an investment by the owners of five hundred dollars that incorporates to manufacture a new drug. It is unlikely that the owners could shield their personal assets from a future lawsuit. Someone who is harmed as a result of taking the drug would very likely be able to "pierce the corporate shield," and make a claim against the individual shareholders. This is because they have inadequately "capitalized" the business for its business purpose.

For most very small businesses, an initial investment of between five to a hundred thousand dollars would show the proper intent to adequately capitalize the firm.

The second problem is with intermingling of assets or affairs. It is perfectly legal for a sole proprietorship or partnership to run its business out of the owner's personal checkbook, and for the owner to use personal and business assets interchangeably (as long as the percentage of use is shown for tax purposes). In the case of a corporation it is critical that the business have a separate checking account and treat all aspects of that corporation as distinct from the owner's personal activities.

The owner must account for any financial transaction between himself and the corporation, including payment, loans, or sales of assets from one to the other. The corporation must be seen in all ways to be a separate and distinct entity from the owner. If not, there is the potential for creditors or judgment holders to "pierce the corporate veil" (show that no real separate entity existed) and go after the shareholders' personal assets.

Taxing authorities will also have problems with mingled accounts and assets. By failing to clearly distinguish between those things that are owned personally and those that are owned by the corporation, management risks losing depreciation allowances and other tax advantages.

Raising cash is another major advantage of the corporation. Through the sale of shares, the corporation can raise capital from outsiders at any time. Each time the company sells additional shares, the current shareholders lose a percentage of their ownership. This is referred to as dilution. However, it is not uncommon for the remaining percentage to be worth more than the larger undiluted share. This would be because of the additional capital that was raised by the sale of stock.

It isn't possible just to sell stock in a corporation any way you see fit. There are many rules as to how to proceed. The states are the only entities that have the right to grant corporate status. Therefore, each state establishes its own rules concerning how the corporation is formed and what procedures must be followed to sell stock.

Corporations may also borrow money from institutions or individuals. Very small businesses usually document these borrowings in the same way that individuals would. They use a standard loan agreement. For larger companies or amounts, the corporation can issue bonds. As with stocks, these securities can be issued only according to rules established by the state in which the company is incorporated or in which the corporation wishes to sell the bonds.

If your business becomes successful, you'll undoubtedly be looking for ways to deprive Uncle Sam and other taxing entities of as much of your money as you can legally achieve. The corporation is the easy winner in this department.

Later sections of this book will detail some of the more complicated profit-sharing, pension, and retirement plans. Many of these are available only to corporations.

In regular "C" corporations, the company, not the individual, pays taxes on its earnings. If the corporate tax rate is lower than the rate the owners would have had to pay, the owners are able to shield themselves from taxation. The business may "retain" earnings up to a point that the taxing authority believes reasonable for that type of enterprise. If the company keeps holding these tax-sheltered earnings beyond this "reasonable" level, the government will treat any additional earnings as if they had been distributed to the shareholders. The corporation must then pay taxes on these amounts.

This is where the double taxation of the "C" corporation comes in. Whether the earnings are actually distributed (in the form of dividends) to the shareholders *or* deemed to be distributed, the shareholders must now pay taxes on this income. The corporation pays tax on the income. Now the owners are taxed on what is left.

It may seem as though this would never be a good idea. However, there are ways to avoid this double taxation. The working owners may pay themselves a "reasonable" salary and bonus. This is deductible to the corporation. You may be able to take all or almost all the profits of the "C" corporation as salary. It may be more than you think you are worth and still be seen as reasonable.

You can capitalize the company with the minimum amount you believe is "reasonable." If the company needs more money, you can lend your own funds to the corporation. The interest you earn is deductible to the company. Later you can pay back the loan. Of course, this principle passes back to you without tax. If you had capitalized the corporation at a higher level instead of using this loan technique, you would not have received tax-advantaged interest. Additionally, if you wanted to take out your original capital it might be seen as a dividend. In any case it would require the transfer of stock that would reduce your ownership if there was more than one owner.

The corporation can also lend you money. All these loans need to be clearly documented, and the company must charge you reasonable interest. However, once again you have been able to take some of the retained earnings out of the company without being taxed.

In many cases, the very small business is better off with a "Sub S" corporation, so called because it falls under Subsection S in the federal tax code. This form combines the advantages of a corporation with those of a partnership.

As long as the owners follow the rules of the federal tax code and their local state corporation code, the company will receive all the benefits of limited exposure offered to the "C" corporation. "Sub S" companies may also take advantage of some of the tax-advantaged pension, profit-sharing, and retirement plans enjoyed by a "C" corp. Others are not available.

The exciting part of the "Sub S" is the elimination of double taxation. In this form, a company passes through its earnings or losses to its owners. The corporation itself pays no taxes. (Actually, some states have a special tax for "Sub S" companies.)

Businesses that are expecting losses often use this form so that the owners can write off these losses. This is not possible in a "C" corp. If you have ten owners holding 10 percent each, and the company loses $100,000, each owner can write off $10,000 (as long as they have invested at least $ 10,000).

Be careful, however. If you have stockholders, or even if you are the only stockholder, a profit will result in a taxable event for all the owners.

This is true whether or not the company pays out any cash (called distributions in a "Sub S"). For instance, if the company above makes $100,000, each shareholder will have $10,000 in regular income for that tax period. If she pays 25 percent tax, she will owe $2,500. If the company doesn't pay out at least that amount, the taxpayer will still owe it. . . and will have to pay it out of pocket.

It's possible to switch your enterprise type. You can do so almost as often as you wish. Of course, each change means costs in money, time, and paperwork. It's not uncommon for a company to start out as a simple sole proprietorship with commingled bank accounts and assets. As the business grows, it may move to separate its affairs from those of its owner. Down the road there may be a need for a working and/or financial partner, at which time the partnership form may be used.

As the company becomes successful and begins to accumulate assets, the partners may feel it is time to incorporate. They might start out as a "C" corporation, but later desire the tax benefits of the "Sub S."

Unless you are a tax expert, you should probably get some advice from a CPA or an attorney as to which enterprise form best meets your needs now. You will also want to ask that question again from time to time as your business grows and changes.

Add to your business plan the enterprise type that you will use, the reasons for so choosing, your planned initial capital, and a list of partners or shareholders, if any.

See the online update on "C" vs "S" vs LLC. **https://WhenFridayIsntPayday.com** Look for page 139

Part 2
Business Licenses and Regulations

You will usually need a business license. This is a requirement of the city or county where the firm will be located. You will almost certainly need this license if you plan to operate out of a commercial facility such as a storefront, office building, or warehouse. You may not need a business license if you have a home-based business that provides professional services, such as a manufacturers' representative or business consultant, or if you are part of a multilevel organization.

When you begin to research your location, you'll see the major disparity in business climate from city to city or county to county. Some are very eager to have businesses of your type locate in their area. You may be bringing jobs for their citizens and additional tax revenues for their coffers. In these cities you may find that getting a license is a ten-minute exercise in filling out a form and paying a small (under one hundred dollars) fee.

Other cities exhibit an antibusiness attitude. In these jurisdictions you may find yourself wading through a substantial bureaucracy before being issued your license. This might include a site inspection by the building department and/or the fire department. You may be required to prove financial standing. You may be provided with a list of dos and don'ts concerning signs, parking, carpooling, hours of operation, and much more. You may also find the initial fee to be abnormally high.

The hoops through which you may have to jump at the city or county level also depend on the type of business you plan to open. Most retailers, wholesalers, and service providers won't be faced with major red tape.

However, if you intend to open a restaurant, manufacturing company, or auto repair business, the story will be quite different. You will find legal requirements and restrictions on everything from the type of materials and equipment you can use to the number and size of restrooms you must provide. These rules and regulations may affect your decision on location. Therefore, you should check out the requirements of likely cities for your type of business before you begin to seek a location.

Because of the endless list of regulations, their common

appearance of arbitrariness, and the low likelihood of enforcement, it is common for business owners to press forward with their plans without carefully evaluating those parts of the local laws that may apply to them.

Clearly, there are plenty of small business owners who know the laws and interpret them in the most favorable light given what they want to accomplish. While not taking a position on the ethics involved at this juncture, I'll simply say that it is good business practice to make such decisions carefully.

For example, a major retail headache today is sign rules. You are paying a great deal of money for a great location, and you want to be able to shout your store name or other message from your walls, window, and rooftop. Most cities now have lists of rules concerning what you can and cannot do in this regard.

The most practical approach to planning your signage in this environment would be to read a copy of the local sign code before you begin thinking about a possible design. Hopefully, you or your sign maker will be able to conceive of a sign that will accomplish your goals within the rules of your city.

If not, you are faced with a choice. You can go to the city with your plan and ask for a variance. Depending upon the city and the type of variance you are seeking, you may or may not be successful. Your other option is to go ahead with your sign and see what happens. This is dangerous because you risk trashing an expensive sign. On the other hand, the violation may go unnoticed or unenforced for years.

If you know that you will be operating in a gray area where it is unclear how the ordinance is intended, *and* you feel it is very important to your company to push into this gray area, you should probably do so without asking the city first. Bureaucrats are predisposed to say no. They also like to bog you down in endless paperwork and commission meetings. If you are truly operating in a gray area, try to avoid this messy and expensive process.

CHAPTER

4

The Grand Opening

The balance of this section and the entirety of the next section deal with the beginning of your business. Many of you are purchasing or taking over an existing business. Thus the business will not be experiencing its grand opening or its first week. However, it will still be *your* beginning, and you'll be encountering a lot of things for the first time. Therefore most of the following applies as much to you as it would to a start-up.

There are two kinds of grand openings. One is a special promotion called a "Grand Opening." If you've established a business that depends on walk-in traffic, you'll undoubtedly want to use your opening as an excuse to have a grand-opening promotion. Whatever you do, *don't do this on your first day.* You'll have plenty of time to do this promotion after you've worked out the kinks of your operation and had enough time to properly plan such an event.

The other grand opening *is* your first day of business. This chapter deals with the second type of grand opening. Put on your seat belt. You are about to begin the ride of your life.

Part 1 Last-Minute Checklist

Wow! If you'd only known it would be this much work just to get to opening day! Let's check off the list of things you should have done before opening your doors for the first time.

1. Created a simple business plan that includes your mission statement, your strategy, and your budget.
2. Secured a location.
3. Contacted vendors for the products and services you will need and established their willingness to supply you.
4. Hired the necessary staff for the opening.
5. Determined the business form you will use and taken care of the necessary legal requirements to establish the business.
6. Secured the necessary government licenses, permits, etc. At the top of the list would be business license, sales tax permit, tax ID number, and any special licenses or permits specific to your type of business.
7. Purchased and installed the necessary equipment and fixtures. You may need to plan the purchase and installation of your phone, fax, and computer lines months in advance. It is a complicated and time-consuming project.
8. Opened a checking account and established a banking relationship.
9. Secured firm delivery dates for your opening inventory. Don't forget forms, stationery, and other incidentals necessary to the conduct of business (such as pens).
10. Established contact with potential customers or clients through advertising, mailings, or personal calls to let them know you are about to open.
11. In some instances, you may wish to have secured orders or contracts in advance of opening.

12. Create online presence at GoogleMyBusiness, Yelp, and created a website.

13. Determined your operating procedures: such things as hours, pricing procedure, purchasing method, invoicing procedure, terms and conditions of sale, warranties and guarantees, return authorizations, bookkeeping system, and filing.

14. Established your e-mail information. Set up your website and business profile on search engines and other services that direct customers to your Web site.

Let me guess that you were doing just fine until number 13. While no amount of planning will result in every base being covered on day one, there is much you should do to appear professional and to avoid losing sales and profit needlessly.

Part 2 Operating Procedures

HOURS OF OPERATION

Now it is time to make a decision. You don't want to needlessly limit your hours of operation. However, you can only personally work so many hours per day. An employee can be hired to expand the number of hours the business is open. However, there is a cost for that. You'll want to carefully evaluate whether there is enough business during those times to justify the wages and other overhead costs incurred by staying open.

You may be able to substantially expand your hours of availability to your customers with voicemail, your smartphone, online stores, e-mail, Skype, your Web site and your presence all over the Web. Every time I've started a new business, my first business card has included my home phone or cell phone. I probably haven't received more than a few dozen calls at home as a result, but it sends a message about my commitment to serving my customer.

PRICING PROCEDURE

Again, we have had some discussion earlier about how to price. Retailers generally need to double cost for items under twenty dollars. Service companies generally must triple their labor cost. Wholesalers look for average margins around 30 percent. Whatever approach you use it is important that, before opening, you formalize your pricing policy. This should be done in such a way that anyone involved in sales or invoicing knows exactly what to do.

Pricing includes discounting. Are you going to offer discounts for volume, cash terms, or to match the competition? If not, you will want to provide your sales team with a rationale for "why not." For instance, you might prefer a one-price-fits-all policy. Customers who want to place large orders may feel that they deserve a price break, but you can tell them that your policy ensures that an even larger competitor will not be able to buy better than they did.

Whatever your pricing and discounting policy, it needs to be formalized. Put it in writing. Discuss it with each person who will have contact with customers or billing. Provide them with the necessary resources to double-check a price if the normal system (price sticker, computer, etc.) isn't available.

PURCHASING

If all goes well, by day two or three you'll need to start reordering some items. First, you'll need to establish the criteria that determine when it's appropriate to reorder. Generally, this is a function of cost, volume of usage, order minimums, lead time, and terms.

You might sell 5 drinking glasses per day that cost you fifty cents each, that take three weeks from order to delivery and must be ordered in fifties. Since it takes three weeks for delivery, you might want to maintain a maximum inventory of twenty-one days (assuming seven selling days per week) times 5 glasses, or 110. In addition, you could establish a standing order for 50 glasses each ten days. If you didn't experience a major variation in your usage, you would range between 60 and 110 in stock.

Other things could radically change this formula. You may average 5 per day, but the most common order size is 100. In this case, you may wish to maintain at least 200 in stock and another 100 on order. This way you'd rarely miss a sale due to being out of stock. On the other hand, your customer may be used to waiting two or three weeks for this type of product. In this case, you may only wish to order the next 100 each time you sell 100 or more.

Your supplier may also offer discounts for volume either in the form of a direct off-price discount or through free freight for purchases above a certain size. Some suppliers offer dating terms (buy now, pay in sixty, ninety, or more days) at certain times of the year. This may allow you to carry more inventory than usual.

In any case, you need to establish a policy as to who orders what. This can be by product category, amount of purchase, or other criteria, but it is extremely important that someone has the responsibility and the authority to order more product. This should be one of the most systematic aspects of your business. Some items might need to be monitored daily, others weekly, and some only monthly or as a special need arises.

The other side of purchasing policy has to do with follow-up. You'll learn soon enough that not all vendors will ship as promised. It may take longer and/or you may not get everything you ordered. This can result in lost sales and major aggravation. Call the vendor the day after you place the order to confirm the availability and ship date. In critical situations, call again on the day before shipment to confirm that the product will be leaving on time and in the quantities promised. Someone needs to be responsible for this follow-up.

INVOICING PROCEDURE

The way you invoice your customer reflects on your entire business. Other than the business transaction (product or service) you provide, the sales slip may be the only lasting impression you'll make, even if this is virtual.

From your first day of business, you should be providing a professional sales slip, personalized with your company name. If you're a retailer, your sales register receipt should have your name on it. If you're using handwritten receipts, don't use standard forms from the local stationery store. Have forms printed with your name on them.

Manufacturers and wholesalers should always use computer-generated invoices on custom invoice paper. Make certain that your pricing is clear. Make it obvious what your terms are. If you want your customer to take the early-pay discount, compute it for them so they can see the actual amount saved. Point out the date by which payment must be received to earn this discount.

Make certain that your customer gets the invoice . . . and *fast.* You should send out an invoice the very same day that the product is shipped or the service rendered. The sooner your bill arrives at your customer, the sooner you're likely to be paid. Attorneys, doctors, and accountants are particularly poor about invoicing quickly. My procedure is to invoice all orders received on one day by 11:00 a.m. the following day. All orders shipped that day are invoiced and mailed by 5:00 p.m. that day.

If you ship product to others, always include a packing slip that shows the number of boxes, total units, weight of each box, shipping carrier used, and date of shipment.

It is also a good idea to show who picked the order and who packed it. The packing slip might say "proudly picked by_____ and "proudly packed by _____"

Who will process outgoing orders? What approach will you use to handle these orders? For most companies, it's best to use a two-step approach. First, you create a packing slip. A copy of this is a picking slip. This goes out to production or warehousing. After the order is shipped, the warehouse copy comes back to bookkeeping, who can then create the invoice and any backorder if appropriate.

TERMS AND CONDITIONS OF SALE

When you offer your customers open account (they purchase goods from you now and pay you later) you need to establish when and under what conditions they will pay you. If you ship merchandise to others, you'll have to decide who pays the freight bill and who is at risk while the goods are in transit.

Your decisions on these issues are important from the standpoint of marketing, cash flow, and bottom line. You want to make the terms attractive enough to entice your customer to make the purchase. But, if you give away too much in this area you may quickly run out of cash or end up without profit.

You may wish to be fairly aggressive when you first start out. By this I mean you may wish to be quick to extend open account, allow larger cash discounts, and ship freight prepaid on small amounts. These concessions would all give you a competitive advantage.

Later, as you start hitting your sales goals, you might slowly tighten up these terms. Your eventual goal might be to equal the terms of your competition. This strategy is not for everyone, but has, in my experience, worked well.

Commonly used terms and conditions are as follows (with their definitions).

CIA. Cash in advance. This is most appropriate where the order is for custom products or services. You may also want to use CIA where the creditworthiness of the customer cannot be ascertained before shipment of delivery or service.

L/C. The next best thing to cash in advance is a letter of credit. This is a document provided by the customer's bank, which confirms that the security of the bank is behind the customer. There are many variations of L/Cs. They are most commonly used for international transactions and very large domestic sales. They are expensive and complicated. I avoid their use whenever possible.

If you find that you must use L/Cs due to a requirement by your bank, your customer, or to ensure payment, consult with a knowledgeable export attorney to determine what requirements to insist on. Be prepared to follow the dictates of the L/C in every specific, as each discrepancy that you create will cost you in time and money.

COD. Cash on delivery. This is a well-known term, but there are a few problems that can occur when using this supposedly safe method of payment.

On a custom order, the customer may go out of business or not actually have the cash when the product or service is delivered. To ensure against this, get all or most of your money CIA for custom orders.

The order is shipped, but the check is no good. If you do much COD shipping, you should ask for bank and credit references to reduce this risk. You may also send your COD on the basis of cash or certified check only.

Problems can occur when merchandise is shipped in several cartons. To save the customer money, you put a COD tag on one package for the entire amount. An unscrupulous customer may elect, though, to keep all the packages except the one with the COD tag, which is returned. To avoid this, divide the amount of the invoice by the number of boxes and send out each box with its own COD amount.

DP or sight draft. These are generally used in international situations, but can be used in larger domestic shipments. DP (documents on presentation) or sight draft uses your bank and the customer's bank as the collecting agent for the shipment. After your truck or shipping line provides you with a bill of lading, this document is sent by your bank to your customer's bank along with a document demanding payment. When the payment is made, the customer's bank gives him the bill of lading so that he can claim the freight.

Net terms. If you decide to offer your customer an open account (which provides product or services now for payment later) you'll need to establish what "later" means. The number of days after invoice that you require payment in full is the net date. You may require payment in ten days. Your terms would read "net ten days." Common net terms include ten days, thirty days, sixty days, and ninety days. Extension of credit costs you the use of your money. Therefore you'll want to limit your net terms to the fewest days possible, given competitive pressures.

Cash discounts. You may wish to encourage your customers to whom you extend payment terms to pay you sooner rather than later. This has many advantages, not the least of which is the common maxim that the sooner you are paid the more likely you are to get paid.

The use of cash discounts can substantially speed up payment. For companies offering net thirty, it is very common to offer a 1, 2, or 3 percent discount for payment within ten days. This would read in the case of a 1 percent discount, "1 percent ten net thirty." A 1 percent discount for ten days versus net thirty will usually induce the most creditworthy and liquid companies to pay in ten days. Three percent ten net thirty terms will potentially result in a large percentage of your customers paying early.

Dating and anticipation. As a wholesaler or manufacturer, you may want to induce your customers to stock up in their offseason. They, of course, are reluctant to purchase more than a bare minimum during a time when their sales are low.

Possibly you have a close-out or special purchase situation. You have been able to buy a very large stock of an item at a heavy discounted price. Now it is important that you sell and ship these items because of space or cash considerations.

These and other opportunities may result in the offering of dating terms. Generally, payment is set for more than ninety days and noted by the due date. For example, you might want to sell product for Christmas in July and offer net January 5 terms.

You may need to offer these terms for many reasons, but the extension of this cash deprives you of its use. Therefore, you may want to use anticipation discounts. This means that if your customer pays earlier than the net date he will pay less. Generally, these terms are stated in one of two ways.

Net January 5, 2% anticipation. This would mean that the customer can take off 2 percent for every thirty days before January 5 that he pays. Sometimes you will want to write out these terms longhand: "Net January 5, 2% December 5, 4% November 5," and so on. To encourage early payment, spell out the customer's opportunity in the body of the invoice: "Deduct $74.00 if paid by December 5. Deduct $148.00 if paid by November 5," and so forth.

10th prox. The term " 10th prox" means the invoice is due on the next tenth of the month. A 2 percent 10th prox, sometimes shown as just "2% 10th" (very close to and can be confused with "2% 10"), means that a 2 percent discount can be taken if paid on the next tenth. To add further confusion to this method, it is common to see "2% 10th net 30." This then would mean that if you were invoiced on the eleventh of January, you could take a 2 percent discount if you pay by February 10, but the invoice is due in full anyway on February 11.

The good news with this concept is that you generally can plan for substantial cash around the tenth. The bad news is that nobody wants their product shipped between the first and the tenth.

You can also mix and match the above terms. You might end up with 30 percent cash in advance, 30 percent on delivery, 40 percent net thirty. Or you can make up your own terms. For instance, I once made an arrangement with a toolmaker to pay a thousand dollars per week during production of the tool.

Consignment or flooring. In this situation, you are maintaining ownership of the product while it is at your customer's place of business until it is sold by him. This use is most common when a new product is having a hard time getting placed or when the item being sold is a very big ticket (pianos and organs, for example). After the product is sold, the customer has an agreed- upon number of days to pay for that item.

The following are some commonly used freight terms you should be familiar with.

FOB. This stands for "free on board" and legally means that the shipper transfers the risk of the freight to the customer as soon as he puts it on board a common carrier. Many, if not most, businesses misuse this term to mean that the customer will pay the freight, not the shipper.

Freight Prepaid. The shipper is responsible for the freight bill. Generally, it also means that he doesn't pass the freight charge along to the customer. A variation is "freight prepaid and add." This usage is common with UPS shipments and situations where the customer has no way to pay the freight company on arrival. Therefore the shipper pays the freight bill but adds the amount to the invoice.

Most companies require that their customer buy a certain quantity at one time to qualify for freight prepaid. For example, this might be expressed as freight prepaid on orders over $1,500, freight prepaid on five hundred units, or freight prepaid on truckload quantities.

CIF. International shipments and some domestic transactions might be arranged CIF, which means the selling price includes the Cost of goods, Insurance, and Freight. In this arrangement, the shipper is paying all costs of shipping, handling, and insurance to the customer's port.

Freight allowance. In this situation, the shipper offers to pay some of the freight. You can show this as a percentage discount, an amount per pound, or merely a negotiated amount.

Freight collect. Here, the customer pays the entire freight bill. Generally, the customer also picks the carrier.

Freight allowed. I've left this one until last because it is rarely used. However, it is my favorite and the one we used at AC International. This means we ship the merchandise freight collect (or prepaid and add in the case of UPS), but the customer may subtract this charge if paid within the net credit terms. The advantage here is that we do not end up with the additional handling of freight bills to pay, and it encourages our customers to pay their bill on time.

Generally, freight-allowed terms will have limitations similar to freight prepaid terms, such as minimum order quantities.

Your terms do not have to apply to everyone equally, although there are some fair-trade regulations concerning equal pricing and terms to customers that would be judged equal. I have used almost every term shown above to cover individual situations.

WARRANTIES AND GUARANTEES

You have been open a few days when a customer calls or comes in. He is hopping mad! His aluminum siding is sliding. Her buttons have popped. The braces are broke. The permanent wasn't.

You need to have a clear policy as to what you will do when your product or service doesn't perform as promised. You also need some idea what your policy will be when you and the customer don't agree on whether the product is the problem or what service was intended.

For many of you there are probably industry standards that will help you with this. However, you need to find out what these are. Call an industry association to see if they can help. If not, see if your suppliers have some ideas. Finally, you may want to ask people in the same business as you who don't see you as a competitor.

Write down your policies and put them where your employees can see them clearly. In many instances, you may want to put them where the customer can also see them clearly.

In establishing your return policy consider the law of two hundred. On average, a bad experience with your company will be repeated until it is heard by two hundred potential customers.

RETURN AUTHORIZATIONS

You will not want your customers just returning product to you indiscriminately. It is all too common that a customer will change his mind while your merchandise is in transit. You want to be the one to decide whether or not you will accept a return.

You need to have an RA (return authorization) system. Generally, you will agree to accept returns of defective material, over shipments, or incorrect shipments. There will even be times when you will accept a return of product that the customer decided to return on a whim. Your order desk should be prepared to give the customer a return authorization number (an RA number) for situations such as these.

Of course, you would prefer not to have merchandise come back. Train your staff in methods of persuading customers to keep the mistakes. You may want to offer discounts, longer payment terms, or consignment.

Many customers are now asking permission to destroy or dispose of small amounts of defective material rather than create the expense of shipping and handling. You may wish to authorize this where you are aware of the defect. It may also be appropriate where the amount of money involved is small. However, it may well be worth the extra expense if you need to monitor these defects or if you believe the customer is throwing away perfectly good items.

BOOKKEEPING PROCEDURES

The management system that should have your highest priority after sales is bookkeeping.

Your sales may be excellent, but if you don't invoice them correctly or collect what you've invoiced, you're headed out of business. You buy product at the right price, but if you don't make certain that your supplier invoices you correctly, watch out.

The checking account. It is *critical* that every effort is taken to keep this account up-to-date and accurate. The first step in this process is the use of numbered checks. You may even wish to use checks with two copies. The first copy will be kept in a numerical sequence file after it has been entered (posted) to the disbursements account or check book. Attach the second copy to the invoice it is paying or file it under a non-invoiced category such as rent. Software often helps with these procedures.

You can also achieve most of the above by using a system known as "One-Write." This system is available through Safeguard Business Systems. Find them on the Internet. Many companies now do most or all of their check writing electronically, through banking services or private systems like QuickBooks.

Use a calculator or computer to check your math. Double-check your results by taking an adding-machine-tape total of the numerical copies and comparing that result to the one in the check book (or disbursements journal).

Reconcile your check book with the bank statement as soon as you receive it. Even the best bookkeeper makes an occasional mistake, and all banks do. Catch them quickly before they cause you serious grief.

Much of this work can be much more easily handled through the use of QuickBooks or other similar software. Use an accountant to help you set up your QuickBooks system so that it is right for your business.

You will need to decide who has access to the check book,

who may sign checks, and how many people must sign a check for it to be valid. Golden nugget: ***Only owners should sign checks***. If there is more than one owner, it is much better if only one owner signs most of them.

There are at least three good reasons why only an owner should have check-signing authority. One is very obvious. The easiest way for someone to rip you off in a big way is to allow them to sign checks. If you must sign, and therefore see, every check that goes out the door, you can be reasonably sure that they are all going to legitimate vendors, government agencies, or employees.

Furthermore, you have the last chance to check the accuracy of the bill to be paid, and the payment. You might recall that you've already paid it. You might notice that the cost figure is not what you negotiated. You might catch an incorrect extension.

Finally, it is actually better for your bookkeeper or controller. If they do not have the authority, they avoid the appearance of impropriety if something goes wrong. I might trust my controller totally, but they never have check-signing authority.

FILING

My partner of 28 years has claimed that he is the best filer in the world. He also maintains that his biggest problem is "unfiling." If you maintain a properly designed filing system, and you insist that those who have access to it file things where they belong, you should not have any problems "unfiling."

You'll use your filing system every day whether analog or virtual. You'll need to look up an invoice to prove something was shipped. You'll need a copy of a purchase order to show your supplier how you were overcharged. You'll need to find a copy of a contract, letter, or quotation. You'll want the information now, and you'll want to be able to read it.

Buy a decent filing cabinet. It's better to buy a sturdy used one than a flimsy new one. Set up as much of the filing system in advance as possible. Most types of businesses will begin with an alphabetic file for invoices by customer. You may also like to keep a numerical invoice file as a backup in case the one in the alphabetic file is lost.

You'll want three payables files. One contains receivers (document showing receipt of merchandise by your receiving clerk) attached to purchase orders. This is a temporary file for after you have received merchandise, but before receiving the invoice.

The second payable file is those "to be paid." Generally, you will keep these alphabetically by vendor. You may wish to keep a separate file by date to remind you that a bill needs to be paid. Some companies keep the invoices to be paid in a date file.

The third payable file is "paid." These are generally filed by supplier name in alphabetical order. Most paid payable files have four critical documents attached together: purchase order, receiver, invoice, and check copy.

Every company should have a correspondence file. The computer has caused many folks to stop keeping hard-copy correspondence files, relying instead on the computer memory. Important letters should be kept in hard copy, too.

A new file is the email file. We keep ours by the month for general correspondence divided by incoming and outgoing in date order. We also keep separate files for those with whom we have a large amount of email correspondence.

You'll need a file for legal documents. The more important ones should also be kept off premises in a safety deposit box. Copies of these plus the less important ones need to be kept close at hand.

This is by no means an exhaustive list of every possible file you may need. Hopefully it will stimulate you to carefully consider the kinds of files you'll need to keep. Again, additional information may be available by calling someone in a similar business.

CREDIT CARDS

For the retailer or Web-based business, credit cards are a necessity. For business-to-business companies such as wholesale, manufacturing, or business services, the credit card is now part of the marketing strategy for most such concerns.

In order to have your own credit card account, so that you can process your customer's credit card, you actually have to have good credit yourself. Be prepared for a rigorous assessment of your credit standing prior to being signed up. If your credit is not very good, or if you are new in business, you will have to pay a premium in charges for processing. There are processing companies who take the riskier accounts and charge for that risk. Your bank may be able to help you find one.

You can also sometimes get a better rate if you go through an industry association or through the National Association of Small Businesses. You can also go through a Web-hosting service. This can be very expensive.

Compare the prices of the various services just like you would the charges for a cell phone or insurance carrier. There can be very considerable savings by doing some research.

Part 3 Last-Minute Attitude Check

"We're alive, partner!" This exclamation is the theme of a movie called *One Good Cop*. It was Michael Keaton's victory cry each time he and one of his partners would narrowly avoid death or worse. During the next three to five years, maybe even longer, you may want to keep that phrase in mind as your business experiences its own close calls.

Keaton's character had the right attitude. Every time he was knocked down, he got up and kept going. Your attitude will have more to do with your ultimate success than any other single thing. I believe you should develop the following attitudes.

1. You must expect success. You can't be satisfied with merely hoping for it. You must set aside your doubts. You haven't elected to take this journey with the idea that if it's too hard, or takes too long, or isn't quite what you'd expected, you'll just toss in the towel. You need to make a personal commitment to see this enterprise through to success.

2. You must be prepared for failure. *"What?!"* you say. "How do you square that with your last comment?" You will fail. Hopefully, the failure will only be temporary and won't bring about the failure of the entire business. Through failure, we learn. Success teaches us little. To the extent that you are mentally and emotionally prepared to fail, you'll be able to take failure, large and small, in stride. If you aren't, your inability to handle failure may result in the total loss of your enterprise.

3. You must conquer fear. If it weren't for fear, every one of us would have already achieved every goal we could ever have imagined. Fear holds us back. For instance, you may really think hot air ballooning would be fun. However, your fear keeps you from trying it.

In business, your fear will keep you from calling on that major account that could put you in the black. Maybe you've called on the account and made your presentation, but now fear is keeping you from calling to see if a decision has been made.

Fear will keep you from taking advantage of opportunities that cross your desk. A little fear might be a good thing to the extent that it keeps one from chasing every opportunity in sight. However, many businesspeople become paralyzed by such fears as adding to their line, computerizing their accounting, or selling overseas.

4. You must quash negative emotions. No one wants to buy from a negative person or work for one. Negative

people don't even really want to be around themselves. Negativism gets in the way of getting things done. Does this mean that we should all walk around with a Pollyanna attitude? Not necessarily, although it surely would be preferable to its opposite. Realism is important. Negativism is not realism.

5.　　　You must make goals. Daily, monthly, yearly sales goals are critical. Cash goals and purchasing goals are essential. If you run out of cash or product, what benefit are the sales? Business improvement goals should be laid out daily, maybe even hourly, as you see flaws that need mending or opportunities that need exploiting.

6.　　　Prepare yourself *every day* to meet the challenges of that day with enthusiasm and decisiveness. If you don't start the day that way, events will control you rather than be controlled by you. At the end of the day, in the evening at home, or first thing in the morning, write lists of the things you need to deal with today along with sober thoughts on how you will do so. Then hit the ground running.

The days that I arrive at the office with less than total excitement usually end the same way. But, on those days when I'm ready for bear, by the end of the day I've usually bagged my trophy.

Extra content MUST READ. Doing the Hard Things. Find it at **https://WhenFridayIsntPayday.com**　Look for page 160

Part 4　The Dress Rehearsal

This section is for those companies who will be meeting the public and have more than one employee, such as retailers, restaurants, service providers, doctors, and wholesalers offering counter service.

It's very important that you appear to know what you're doing from the very first day. To help produce that result, you may wish to schedule a dress rehearsal. It will cost you an extra day's pay for your employees, but it will almost surely be worth it.

Prepare everything as if you were ready to open on rehearsal day. Invite your spouse, neighbors, friends, supplier salespersons to come in and play the role of customer.

Ask them to really put you to the test. Some should be demanding. Others totally passive. Try one customer at a time, and a houseful. Pay special attention to whether everything is clear to your "customers." How were they treated by your people? Did the person writing up the bill know what he was doing? How about credit card handling?

Have someone bring back a damaged product. Have people call the store to see how your people handle the phones. Run through your opening and closing procedures.

You may believe that you can do this just as well with real customers, but your mind will be going a million directions at once during the business day. By acting as a director at a dress rehearsal, you can fine-tune your business operations while focusing on just this aspect of your operation.

Part 5 The First Day

As you approach the building on day one, your first balloon is popped. People are not lined up waiting to get in. On entering, you find there is no voicemail, and two hours later the only call you receive is from your spouse asking how it's going. As the first day ends your revenues are just under ten bucks. A quick glance at your budget shows that your expenses for that day were closer to two-hundred.

Now is not the time to question what went right or wrong. The fact that anybody bought anything from you today may be a great sign. The question you should be looking at is, "What did I do today? How did I spend my time?"

If you spent a great deal of the time watching traffic go by, doing useless paperwork, or checking Facebook, you should probably update your resume on Indeed and Linkedin.

During this start-up period, every minute of time that is not being devoted to a project essential to keeping the doors open must be spent selling, promoting, and planning promotion. Only one of those things you may be planning as a promotion is a future grand opening. Many businesses have no need of such an event or cannot gain from it. Others such as ad agencies or beauty shops may want to hold an open house where potential clients enjoy a few snacks and admire your new facility.

If you're in retail, take ten-minute breaks (with a note on the window "back in ten minutes") to pass out brochures in the neighborhood. Don't stand in your doorway and look sadly at the passers-by. Be bold, forget fear. Invite them in for a cup of coffee. Give them a coupon for a 10 percent discount next time they come.

Rent a clown outfit and stand in front of your place of business to attract attention. Hire a mariachi band to play in your front window.

When should you start taking all these drastic actions? *From the first day.* You have expenses. Those expenses don't stop and wait for sales. Each day you don't sell enough to pay those expenses puts you one day closer to an unacceptable result of all your hard work and money: going broke!

How should you spend your first day if you are a wholesaler, broker, manufacturer, or sales rep? On the phone, in your car, or on an airplane. You have to be in front of the decision makers. You can spend all your time fine-tuning your equipment, counting your inventory, or meeting with vendors and principals, but none of those activities is going to result in a sale. You need sales! *Now!*

How about service providers such as doctors, lawyers, and CPAs? It is the rare professional who isn't uncomfortable about "selling" his services. It hasn't been so long since such action was considered unethical or even illegal.

Such is not the case today. The day-to-day overhead expenses of most professionals are among the highest of very small businesses. Besides, each hour that a lawyer or doctor isn't practicing, the lost opportunity cost of doing so as an employee is very high.

First, contact every other member of your profession in your area to offer your services to them. Doctors can commonly benefit from referrals of other doctors who have too large a caseload or who don't practice in your specialty. Ad agencies may be able to pick up small clients from other agencies. What is an unprofitable business to one company may be life and death to a start-up?

Restaurateurs, go out and visit every owner and manager of a business anywhere nearby. Give them a free lunch coupon or two. If your food is good, they will pay for that free lunch many times when they return with employees, customers, and suppliers.

Join local service and professional clubs, the chamber of commerce, charities, or the boosters for the high school. Meet people. Hand out cards.

Visit or call companies with which you have potential synergy. Contractors should leave their cards at the local lumberyards and hardware stores so that a do-it-yourself can get a lead for the times he is in over his head.

If you are opening a family counselling center, you'll want to leave your card with area pastors, doctors, school nurses and counsellors, and social service providers.

If you're renting cars, you should be contacting insurance agents, claims adjusters, body shops, auto repair facilities, and hotels.

The negative guys are piping up: "I sell manufactured products to wholesalers. After I've called every one twice in the same week, what is left for me to do to help my sales?"

1. Go out and call on the retailers that they serve. Do this on your own or with one of their salesmen if possible. Sell product direct to these retailers if you don't already have distribution in that area or take their order and give it to your

customer to ship.

2.   Set up a meeting with a group of end users of your product. Find out what you can do to make the product more appealing. Ask them to use the product and come back to you with testimonials. Offer to give them free product in exchange for their help.

3.   Offer one or more of your customers a discount on product if they will send out your brochure in one of their mailings. The fastest turnaround would be in a packing slip or invoice.

4.   Offer free product to your wholesaler if she will include the free one in each shipment she makes to a customer.

5.   Send out the craziest low-cost advertising piece you can think of. We have seen brochures rolled up in tubes, mailed in a bottle, or delivered by FedEx. Do anything to get noticed.

Let me throw out one more example. Then you should be able to devise a similar list for your business. Let's say you are a photographer.

1.   Call others in the wedding business near you. The Tux rental shop, the bridal gown retailer, the baker, and the videographer. Especially call all the wedding venues near you. Set up meetings with each one and discuss sharing contacts.

2.   Go on Linkedin and take a look at the photos of executives you know. If some don't look too attractive, call and offer a free sitting to create a professional headshot that will improve their image. This contact may lead to photos for brochures and advertisements.

3.   Leave your card with the best four-by-six color picture of a baby you have ever taken at the local baby furniture store, each toy store, and with every OB/GYN in town. Offer the manager or owner a 10 percent commission for anybody he sends your way. If you don't get anything in a week, offer a 20 percent commission.

4.   Go talk to the manager of the fanciest restaurant in your area. Suggest that she let you take pictures of the patrons. By the time they finish eating you would provide them with a

five-by-six color photo encased in a folder with the restaurant's logo on the front. Keep the price reasonable, but get the couple's name and address. Follow up with a brochure that tells of all your services. Then offer to do food shots for the owner.

5.   Go to local advertising agencies and offer to do their next photo shoot for free. (They pay only for materials, not your time.) You risk one day in exchange for the potential for much future business.

Sell ■ Promote ■ Sell ■ Promote ■ Sell ■ Promote ■ Sell

That is your job and virtually your only job during business hours until you are covering your nut (expenses). Clearly, if you are the one who provides the service, or you must create the product, ship it, and so on, you will have to take care of these things as well. As much as is humanly possible, however, do these things at night during this critical start-up time. Sell during the day, run your machinery at night. Sell during the day, type invoices at night, box and ship before eight o'clock in the morning.

Some of you may be able to reverse the process. For instance, doctors, lawyers, printers, travel agents, and other service providers must generally perform their professional services during business hours. However, they should use dead time, lunch hours, evenings, and Saturdays to find folks to sell.

Evenings also provide time for creating brochures, sending follow-up emails, and planning sales calls. Your family is going to scream that you work all the time. Explain to them that if you work very, very hard now, you should be able to slack off later. If you ease up now, you may be fighting for your business life for years.

Part 6 Surviving the First Week

Are we having fun yet!? Did you hit your sales goal for the week? Have you screwed something up real good yet? Have you had enough nos to last a lifetime? Is your family still basically supportive of your decision to get out on your own? The correct answers to the above should be: "Not quite," "almost," "yes," "I'll get over it," and "hanging in there." Those answers would mean that you have what it takes to make this work.

The first week is tough. Unless your business is very special, you already need a vacation. What those questions were designed to elicit is:

A.   Do you still have a positive mental attitude?

B.   Did you set your sales goals unrealistically low or high, or did you set them at all?

C.   Have you been actively going after business, trying things, taking risks? There is no truer statement that "If you're not screwing up, you're not doing anything."

D.   If you haven't faced rejection this week, you either haven't asked for the order or you're seriously under-pricing your product. In most cases, the incorrect answer here means you haven't even called on any customers.

E.   If your family is already nervous, anxious, angry, or all three, you haven't properly prepared them. Sit down today and have a heart-to-heart talk. Be totally and completely honest about your feelings at this time, and about the sacrifices they are facing.

It is now Sunday night. Tomorrow starts a new week. Don't be alarmed or concerned if you don't sleep well tonight. Your adrenaline will keep you going. This next idea took me over twenty-five years of sleepless nights to develop. You may already know about it, but if not, it could be the extra 1 percent advantage you'll need to succeed.

Get out your legal pad, notebook, computer, or whatever you use to write notes, scribble down ideas, or doodle while on the phone. Get a clean sheet and write the next day's day and date in big letters at the top. Start from the first line on the page and write down as many things as you can think of that you need to do, could do, or should do tomorrow ... or soon.

Here is an example of one of my to-do sheets.

Monday, May 6

1. Follow up with Paul regarding his call at Schwinn.
2. Rent must be paid today.
3. Call Tony about his new product: Price, minimum quantity, terms.
4. Make sales calls on Fisher, Nike, and C & G.
5. Call Jim at Bill's wholesale to see how he liked the samples.
6. Make sure the samples went out to Custom House and Denver Sales.
7. Check inventory on neon orange water bottles. Also white.
8. Where is that promised order from Midwest Distributors?
9. Do we have everything we need to start the Kmart order?
10. Get Mr. Tuffy brochure printed.
11. Redo May's sales goal based on shipments last week and orders in house.
12. Promise Kodak their shipment by Tuesday.
13. Need two extra temporaries from the service tomorrow.
14. See when bookkeeper will have April profit-and-loss.

Here is what the list is going to do for you.

1. Compiling the list during a quiet time on Sunday night—or any night for that matter—provides a chance to let the great computer between your ears digest information and foster creativity. You'll think of things in this environment that you won't come up with any other way. New products, approaches, and solutions will just pop into your mind.

2.   You now have a list to go by. It'll allow you to work very rapidly on the things that are most important. Some specialists in the science of lists believe that you should go back over the list and create priorities. That may work for you. I prefer to scan the list several times per day and select those items that seem most appropriate for that moment.

3.   As you complete an item on the list, scratch it out. There is a terrific psychological uplift to that action. As the page gets darker and darker with lines crossed out, your satisfaction level goes up and up.

4.   There is something about writing it down. When you write down these activities, there is more of a feeling that they must be done. Therefore, the less appealing items, once written down on a to-do list, are more likely to get done, and sooner.

5.   Finally, having written all of this down clears and settles your mind. This will go a long way toward helping you sleep, even when you are faced with enormous pressure.

How are your time-management skills? Check out the extra online material available on improving your time management. Go to **https://WhenFridayIsntPayday.com**   and look for page 168.

CHAPTER

5

The First Month

BELIEVE IT OR NOT, the bruises will heal, it will get worse before it gets better, and you will see your children again. If these are not some of the things you are currently thinking about, you aren't working hard enough to make it. During this period of your business's development, you need to be as devoted to it as you were to your spouse on your honeymoon ... as devoted as a mother is to a newborn . . . *and for all the same reasons.*

If you're not coming very close to your goals yet, now might be a great time for you to write down your daily schedule—where you go on a particular day and whom you talk to. By engaging in that exercise, you may be able to see where you are poorly allocating time. Wise use of your time in these early days will greatly improve your company's fortunes.

Part 1 Training, Training, and Retraining

The comparison of your month-old business to a newborn doesn't stop with their common need for massive doses of time, energy, and emotion. Both also need constant training and retraining. In fact, a baby may be easier in this regard. One writer claims that infants rarely have to learn the same lesson more than once. This won't be true for your employees. Maybe not even for you.

One aspect of starting a new company that makes training difficult is that you haven't done it before. Thus, as you learn, you need to untrain your employees of the bad habits you had earlier trained them in.

Training should be a daily enterprise. Some management experts suggest a daily meeting for this task. Some suggest you can accomplish great results a minute at a time. My personal preference is to write a short memo that treats the issue, make copies, and disperse them to those who will be affected an hour or so before a meeting announced with the memo. If I believe the meeting will take five minutes or less, I conduct it standing. If longer, sitting. However, the critical issue for me is to keep the meeting on the subject at hand and as brief as possible. I invite questions and comments, but I am not interested in providing grandstanding opportunities for those in the group. There will be plenty of opportunity for that in the looser format of a brainstorming session.

Part 2 Decision Making

One of the most formidable new skills you'll have to learn in the first thirty days or so is how to make a decision. Most who haven't led before haven't had the opportunity, or the burden, of making critical decisions—especially ones where timing is essential. Hence, it's easy to second-guess the decisions you do make. My advice is: **Don't.** Rather, just charge ahead, and do your best to make it work. If it doesn't, park your ego at the door and make another decision: how to solve the new situation.

How *does* one go about making good decisions in a timely manner? The only skill harder to teach is creativity, and they operate similarly. Here is a step-by-step approach that *can* be used by anyone.

STEP ONE

Determine the specific problem or opportunity that needs to be addressed. At least half of decision making is knowing what the problem is, and the problem frequently isn't what it appears to be.

You have an employee who doesn't seem to be cutting it. He appears lazy and disinterested. You have encouraged, admonished, trained, and threatened. Nothing is working. You need to decide whether or not to fire this person.

The problem seems to be that you've made a poor hire. You feel bad about letting the person go. You aren't sure how quickly you can replace him. Right now, he's better than nothing. Take the situation and stand it on its head, shake it around, and turn it inside out. Here are just a few of the possible problems that aren't so obvious that might provide an easy solution.

■ During your attempts at motivation, etc., you never really explained to this person what you expected and/or what he could expect long term.

■ You've been doing a great deal of talking. Have you done any listening? Maybe your employee is going through a difficult time, or has a tendency to say yes to you during training even when he doesn't understand.

■ Is he really better than nothing? Could the rest of your staff fill in until you could find a replacement?

■ Does he have enough specific direction? Some employees need a detailed list of things to do.

■ He hates the work and is staying only because he feels bad about letting you down.

- There really isn't enough to keep him busy.
- He finishes tasks very quickly and therefore appears to be lazy when he doesn't know what to do next.

Do you see that each of these possible problems practically screams its solution? So, step number one is to evaluate the situation from every perspective you can think of and make certain that you have correctly identified the problem.

Many times you'll identify what you believe to be the problem and you'll still be faced with several valid options. In this case, you'll move to step two.

STEP TWO

Gather as much information as you possibly can in the time available. Ask questions of those who are likely to be affected. Give a call to someone who you believe has faced a similar dilemma. Go to the library and bookstore or search the Internet to see what may have been written on the subject. Call your CPA, attorney, or other professional who may have insight into the situation.

A few years ago, our product liability insurance policy was cancelled. This was during one of those times when the commercial insurance companies were losing their shirts. The company who had written our policy decided to get out of commercial insurance altogether. The obvious first call was to an insurance agent, and then another, and another. It soon became clear that the normal method of securing new insurance was not going to work. No one thought we had a chance of getting a policy.

We didn't consider it an intelligent option to remain uninsured. Moreover, many of our customers required that we carry insurance if they were to continue carrying our product. In this case the problem was clearly defined, so step number one in this exercise wasn't going to be any help.

I began seeking information. The problem was nationwide and across all industries. As a result, there were many articles on the subject. I read them all. Any lead that came out of these stories, I followed up.

I called other friends in business. Many still had their coverage. I asked for the names of their insurer and/or agent. I called my CPA and my lawyer for ideas on where to look or how to get around the problem. Sometimes the call resulted in a lead. Sometimes that lead pointed to another source, which yielded yet another possible person who might be able to help. We called suppliers and some customers to ask who insured them.

We researched any potential information that we could think of. One of those calls may have resulted in our finding insurance. It didn't. Thus we went to step three.

STEP THREE

As you do your research, you will, from time to time, want to put your creative juices to work in hopes of turning the information you have gathered into a solution.

There are many ways to do this, but all of them require one thing: allowing your brain to do all the work by itself. Some call it right-brain activity. Others call it alpha. A light bulb going on is the symbol of success in this approach. Prayer or meditation is often quite helpful. Sleeping on it works quite well. In my opinion each works about the same way: After you gather all this information, you tell your brain what you need. Then you forget about it. Think about nothing, as in some forms of meditation. Think about something else entirely, as is commonly the case in an alpha state. But stop searching for an answer, so that your brain can be free to come up with the solutions on its own.

When the ideas start to flow, let them. Don't reject anything at this point. It is very likely that you will get these ideas in the middle of the night, just before you doze off, or right after awakening in the morning. Try to stay in a dreamy state for a while and let the ideas develop. Edison used to hold a glass tumbler in his hand off the edge of the bed. If he dozed off, the glass would fall and wake him up. Then he could continue his idea session.

When you feel that you have everything you are going to get, find a pad and pencil and write your ideas down. As the day progresses some of these thoughts may seem ridiculous, but you will very likely have one or two real gems.

We considered buying out a company that still had insurance. We talked about dropping some of our more obvious insurance problem products. (We were carrying bicycle helmets for infants.) We discussed the only offer we had. The amount would have eliminated any hope for profit that year, but we would have had coverage until the insurance climate changed.

We suggested to some underwriters that we would agree to a large deductible. We called all the vendors who supplied us with raw materials and finished goods. We figured that if every one of them had insurance and could provide us with a certificate of insurance, this might satisfy our customers. We even considered starting a nationwide political movement to change the way product liability was being handled.

We considered becoming a foreign corporation. Consumers rarely sue foreign manufacturers. It is easier to go after the importer, wholesaler, or retailer to whom the foreign manufacturer sells.

We finally made a decision, which in this case was very expensive. We accepted the only offer to cover us that was available. For the next two years we paid 2 percent of all sales to maintain only five hundred thousand dollars in coverage.

STEP FOUR

Now that you have come up with a list of approaches, it is time to pick one. Get as much input as possible from those you trust. Then go for it. By this time you should have a real good gut feeling of which approach is best. Repeatedly I have heard famous leaders talk about the importance of following their gut instincts. But of course those instincts have been honed by first following steps one, two, and three outlined above.

Typically, you are dealing with an issue that has a limited window of opportunity in which to make a decision. I still go through these steps as completely as possible in the time allowed.

If this process seems foreign to you, you may need to go through it very deliberately the first few times you're faced with a major decision. Others will recognize the process as something they do subconsciously all the time.

Dramatically improve your decision making. Join a MasterMind group or form one. For more on this see our online section at **https://WhenFridayIsntPayday.com**   Look for page 175

CHAPTER

6

Months Two Through Six

GONE ARE THE OPENING-DAY JITTERS. You've fumbled your way through the first few weeks. By the end of the month you almost feel as though you and your staff can handle the routine aspects of running the business.

Don't become discouraged by the fact that there are times each day when the unexpected causes a mini-crisis, or even a major one. As long as you are in business, you'll be faced with events you have no control over or which you've had no experience with. Through the use of three-track thinking and the decision-making approaches just discussed, you should be able to deal with each of these crises without needless anxiety.

Now it's time to incorporate some practices that you as the manager will use to help run the business from now until you retire. We'll begin with the most important daily activity you should perform.

Part 1 The Daily Numbers

Business is about people. The better your people, the better you'll do. Business is about selling. Nothing happens until something is sold. Business is about managing. Organization is critical to maximizing profitability. The scorecard for business is numbers.

Golden nugget: *Each day you will want to have a set of statistics that will tell you how your employees are doing and how you are doing as a team.* You will compare some of your employees to each other. You may evaluate some of your company numbers to other similar firms. Most important, you'll want to make evaluations about past numbers, your plan or budget, and your future.

Every business will have some numbers that are unique to them, but there are many that are universal. If you're adept at using a spreadsheet program, you may want to program these daily numbers into your computer so that you can manipulate them.

SALES

This item should be at the top of every list. What were your total sales for the day? What is the total so far this month? How does that MTD (month-to-date) figure compare with your plan for this month?

With these three pieces of information you can start to manage your business. Why were sales today less than you hoped for? Why is the month-to-date figure less than the plan? If these numbers were substantially higher than the plan, should you re-evaluate your plan, or are there reasons why you expect the remaining portion of the month to balance the fast start?

Do today's numbers suggest a need for action? Are you out of a critical material or part? Do you need more people? If yes, should they be permanent or temporary? Should you cut back on your ordering or increase it?

Some companies may benefit from breaking their sales numbers into two categories: orders and shipments. This would be true if you generally have a backlog or back-order situation.

Using this approach, your new orders for the day would help you make decisions about advertising, promotion, selling time, discounts, and effectiveness of your sales force. Shipments give you the data you need to properly manage your manufacturing and shipping departments.

A variation on this theme occurs in service industries where appointments are made, such as doctors, plumbers, and beauty salons. You may want a daily number that would indicate the number of hours of appointments that were booked each day. This would affect your planning concerning hours of operation, advertising and other promotion, and need for additional personnel.

PROFIT

The daily profit number becomes more important when your product mix has a wide variety of margins. In a retail store, you might have some items that you buy for a dime and sell for a dollar. Other products might cost you $300 and you sell them for $330 (I hope not, but I've seen it). In this type of situation a daily gross profit number will allow you to fine-tune your sales effort toward either more gross sales or a higher average margin. Let's consider an example.

You may know that you really need to create more total gross profit per day. You are now producing $150. You need $240. You also know you wouldn't have to hire more salesclerks to sell three more wedding cakes at $330 each. It is unlikely that you'd ever sell one hundred more doughnut holes at $1 each to reach the same $90 in additional profit. Thus, even though your profit margin on the one is only 10 percent versus 90 percent on the other, you need to aim your sales, advertising, and promotion efforts at the 10 percent item

DAILY CASH RECEIPTS

Your daily cash receipts number will tell you whether you're going to have enough cash to pay today's bills (and maybe whether you're going to have anything to take home to your family today). If those receipts aren't what you hoped for, you'll be able to take some kinds of actions to improve them, both short-and long-term.

You may wish to change your terms. If you usually allow net sixty days, you may want to send out a letter informing all or certain customers that as of June 1, your terms will be net thirty.

You may want to prioritize those shipments that will be delivered COD. Another option is to start calling certain customers and offering a discount for faster payment. Or you may want to intensify your collection effort.

ACCOUNTS RECEIVABLE BALANCE

That brings us to the second part of this number, the accounts receivable balance. You'll want to see this number in conjunction with the day's shipments, cash receipts, and the beginning accounts receivable (A/R) balance for the month. It might look something like this:

Beginning A/R-6/1	$ 15,682.00
Shipments 6/7	$ 1,345.00
Cash Receipts 6/7	$ 990.00
Shipments MTD	$ 5,431.00
Cash Receipts MTD	$ 3,806.00
A/R balance – 6/7	$ 17,307.00

If I were to see these numbers on my daily report, I'd want to immediately check my accounts receivable detail. Who owes me what, and is it past due? We'll deal with methods for collection in section 3, but for now the important thing is recognizing that these daily numbers will help you pinpoint the things you need to do. In this case you'd check your A/R detail to see whether a collection effort might improve your daily receipts.

It may turn out that your credit customers are paying you just fine, but your sales in the first seven days of last month were low compared to the last twenty-three days. Therefore your collections should improve as those invoices mailed in the latter part of the month become due.

CHECKING ACCOUNT BALANCE / DISBURSEMENTS

This part of your daily report might look like this:.

Beginning cash 6/7	$ 6,555.00
Payroll 6/7	
Payments to vendors 6/7	$ 4,352.00
Tax payment 6/7	
CODs paid	$ 533.00
Other	
Other ____	
Cash receipts 6/7	$ 990.00
Ending cash 6/7	$ 2, 660.00

You may also want to prepare a similar report that shows these totals on a month-to-date basis. This will allow you to evaluate your expenditures against a monthly plan or budget.

OTHER

Depending on the business you are in you may also want to see such numbers as:

- Sales calls made
- Calls received by order desk
- Daily payroll expense
- Inventory—total or by certain items
- Purchase orders placed—total value of open POs
- New payables—total outstanding payables
- Production—by machine—total value of production
- Backlog—by item—by total value—by days to produce
- Back orders—by item—by total value
- Total presentations made—total converted to orders
- Loan balance—loan available
- A/R over sixty days
- Downtime—by machine
- Capacity utilization—by percent
- Capacity available—by value of lost opportunity

There is a fair amount of time and energy required to compile some of these numbers. You may not have the personnel to do as many as might be useful. Start with sales and, if appropriate, orders. Checking account balance would be second. A/R and disbursement would generally be important where applicable. Most of the rest is very specific to your type of enterprise. Do as many as you can that help you run the business.

Here is an example of a very complete daily report.

	Today	This Week	This Month	Budget
Beginning cash	1,450.98	3,553.76	1,212.78	
Cash receipts	1,700.00	1,895.77	13,375.60	35,000.00
Payroll & tax			1,255.00	5,000.00
CODs	55.00	290.00	1,775.56	5,000.00
Overhead	294.52	294.52	1,350.55	1,500.00
Payables	355.00	1,576.90	5,883.66	15,000.00
Commissions			877.00	2,500.00
Notes paid				1,500.00
Other	870.73	1,712.38	1,870.88	2,000.00
Total disbursed	1,575.25	3,873.80	13,012.65	32,500.00
Ending cash	1,575.73	1,575.73	1,575.73	
Beginning A/R	40,786.97	38,709.24	41,295.00	
Beginning backlog	7,559.90	8,670.55	4,220.55	
New orders	1,456.50	2,619.35	15,963.42	38,000.00
Shipped	2,202.37	4,475.87	13,369.94	37,000.00
Ending backlog	6,814.03	6,814.03	6,814.03	8,000.00
Cash receipts	1,700.00	1,895.77	13,375.60	35,000.00
Ending A/R	41,289.34	41,289.34	41,289.34	
Beginning A/P	35,689.96	33,379.90	29,930.83	
New A/P		3,531.96	11,287.79	16,000.00
Paid A/P	355.00	1,576.90	5,883.66	15,000.00
Ending A/P	35,334.96	35,334.96	35,334.96	

Sales/Salesperson	Backlog	New Orders	New Orders MTD	Shipped MTD
Bob	1,250.97	312.75	4,554.11	4,002.92
Diane	3,378.36	790.98	8,510.65	7,979.22
Art	1,665.56	100.35	1,995.55	1,225.99
Cindy	1,265.01	252.42	903.11	161.81

A quick glance through this daily report would offer insights and trigger a few questions:

A.   Cash receipts are doing fairly well for nine business days. (There would be one weekend by the eleventh.)

B.   You have practically spent your whole budget for overhead. You would want to go back and see what was spent. Then evaluate what is left that you must buy during the balance of this month.

C.   New orders were a bit off yesterday, although you are doing close to projection for the month. It still might not hurt to have a talk with one or more of your salespeople.

D.   A/R seems in reasonably good shape with cash receipts almost equal to shipments for the month.

E.   New A/P is running way ahead. Did you have to purchase this amount of inventory so early in the month? What will you need to purchase during the balance of the month?

F.   Your salespeople seem typical in that there is one star, two solid players, and one laggard. It appears that your laggard is going downhill fast. In addition, she seems to be selling the things you least like to ship. As a result, her backlog is very high compared to her sales. It is probably time to make a switch, especially if Cindy is on payroll and not commission.

Part 2 The Monthly Statements

Income statement. You'll want to produce one every month. Your business can be in big trouble for a long time and you won't even know it without an income statement. We have fully detailed the income statement in section 2, chapter 2, part 6.

Inventory. This is the value of all merchandise that you carry for resale. It does not include office furniture, production equipment, or other items not offered for sale. As mentioned earlier, there are some very sophisticated aspects to placing a value on that inventory.

In addition to the question of how much direct and indirect overhead to include in the value, there are other issues such as LIFO and FIFO. FIFO means first in, first out. If you use the FIFO method you make the assumption that the inventory of items you continuously purchase that are now in your warehouse are those you have most recently purchased. If you use LIFO (last in, first out), you assume that your current inventory is made up of items purchased earlier, and that the items you have recently purchased are sold.

In an inflationary environment the use of FIFO would result in a higher valuation for your inventory. Good for the balance sheet; bad for income tax. LIFO would have the opposite effect.

These and other questions have profit and tax ramifications, and should be discussed in detail with your accountant. All that aside, in evaluating your inventory for the purpose of determining whether you are profitable, you must be consistent. If you change the method of valuation from period to period, you will not have any idea what your profit is.

You may find it costly in terms of time and energy to take a physical inventory each month, but it's usually worth it. You should almost certainly set up a perpetual inventory (in which each sale or receipt of product is recorded and changes your inventory balance immediately). You will achieve excellent advantages from doing one or the other. Your month-end inventory report might look like this.

Item	On Hand	Value	Purchases	Sales	Average YTD
B52	522	570.55	80	120	110
XKE	6	9.00	30	50	30
711	140	280.00	65	70	60
R2D2	50	500.00	0	2	10

The last column, average YTD, means the average monthly sales you have experienced so far this year. There are many other meaningful averages you may like to look at such as average last twelve months or last four months. The first would give you long-term experience with the product. The other might show a trend.

As you look at the information above, the first thing that sticks out is that you are over-inventoried in R2D2s, especially considering how much they cost. The second thing is almost as obvious. You should probably be buying way more XKEs. Your B52s are a little heavy, maybe a sale is in order, but your sales of this item are good, so you don't want to give them away. Product 711 shows an almost perfect example of purchases and inventory in relation to sales.

Gross-profit-margin method of determining profit and loss. You probably won't take an inventory every month. You may not even find the time to take a proper inventory every quarter. However, you'll still want to have a P & L (profit and loss) prepared monthly. You can do this by establishing a normal gross margin for your business. It may take three or four actual inventories to begin to get a handle on this normal amount. Each time you take an inventory, you'll arrive at a gross margin percentage. Soon you'll be able to determine an average for your operation. If you show 45 percent for one period, 52 percent for another, and 46 percent for another, you can just add them and divide by 3.

With this number you can now determine the dollar amount of your cost of sales and your gross profit without taking an inventory. However, it is easy to become deluded when using this method, especially if you don't take an actual—the term is "physical"—inventory for a long time. Maybe you have had to discount more heavily during the period you are using the gross-margin method than you did when you took an actual inventory. Over time, you may begin to add overhead, because according to your P & L you are quite profitable. Then you take an actual inventory only to find out you've been losing money all along.

Another way to avoid this problem is to maintain a perpetual inventory. This means that either by using a computer or a manual method you account for every item sold or bought during the period. In this case you would know the value of your "book" inventory without actually counting it. The reason I refer to this inventory as a book inventory is to differentiate it from a physical inventory. You see, you could still be way off base. Through bookkeeping errors, short shipments by your suppliers, invoicing errors, over shipments by your staff, or outright theft, your actual inventory may be substantially different from your book inventory.

In order of preference, you will want to use physical inventory, perpetual inventory, and, only as a last resort, gross-profit method.

Accounts receivable aging. If you allow your customers to purchase from you on account you will find that not all of them pay you according to terms. In fact, you will likely end up having some customers who take quite a while to pay ... if not forever.

To track the quality of your customers' payments and as an aid to your collection effort you must produce an aging report of your A/R. Generally, it will look like this:

Customer	Current	30-60 Days	61-90 Days	91 days or over	
ACME	380.55	57.95			
B-One			195.49		
Century	549.90				
Dave's				775.90	
E-Plus		88.80			
Falcon	50.50				
Total	**980.95**	*146.75*	**195.49**	*775.90*	2099.09
Percentage	**47%**	*7%*	**9%**	*37%*	100%

By spreading your receivables in this way, you get a picture of your situation with outstanding accounts. ACME, Century, and Falcon are probably okay. B-One needs some attention, but

Dave's is serious. E-Plus is a bit past due, but it is a small amount. The situation with Dave's has even caused your entire aging to be skewed. It is very serious indeed to have 37 percent of your outstanding balances in the ninety-day column.

We will come back to this area in section 3 as we talk about how to collect receivables.

Accounts payable aging. This is done in exactly the same way as accounts receivable aging. With this report, however, you are getting a picture of how well you are paying your suppliers. Use the same chart as above, but change the "customer" heading to "supplier." If Dave's is one of your important suppliers you may be in danger of his cutting you off from open account or even not shipping you at all. By preparing this aging on a monthly basis, you may begin to see trends that indicate you are getting further and further behind in your bills. You will also find it easier to make decisions of whom to pay when you have less than enough to pay everyone.

Sales analysis. With this report you will take a look at how your customers are doing with you. You can divide this by salesperson. You will be looking for trends and opportunities. This report can be formatted in many different ways. This is my particular favorite:

SALESPERSON #556

Customer	Sales	YTD	Same Month Last Year	YTD Last Year	Total Last Year
Falcon	535.25	1,045.90	135.55	388.50	947.95
ACME	165.47	644.12	676.90	948.88	1,778.33
Dave's		549.24	70.70	510.76	887.32
Century	98.50	220.11			
E-Plus	40.65	40.65	489.44	838.91	2,772.98
B-One		10.50		21.00	42.00
Total	836.87	2,510.52	1,372.59	2,709.05	6,428.58

You can probably already see how helpful this report would be. This particular salesperson is down in her sales year to date versus last year. She was also off this month compared with the same month last year. In fact, she is down more for the month than she was year to date. It may be that she just had a bad month, but it bears careful evaluation next month.

You will note that this format lists the accounts in order of best customer by sales, YTD. This allows me to see who my best customers are. In this case clearly Falcon is coming on strong, but E-Plus has fallen way off. Why didn't Dave's order this month? Better to check now than to find out two or three months from now that he has switched to the competition. It may affect ordering patterns and it is easier to get him back if you call him soon after the decision was made to switch.

Other sales reports that could be valuable include item sales by customer, order frequency by customer, or profit margin by customer.

There are many other reports that are useful to certain industries. Restaurants may want to keep track of the number of times they turn their tables per day or per meal. They might also track waste percentage. Job shops should be interested in machine utilization analysis both by number of hours of production and value of production. Lawyers and accountants may want to know the percentage of billable to non-billable hours worked by each partner and associate. Consider what information would be important for you to monitor monthly. Check with consultants or trade associations in your business category to see what others do.

Part 3 Dealing with Crisis

The balance of section 2 is devoted to the most likely emergencies and near emergencies that may develop in the first weeks and months after you open. Each will be followed by a variety of solutions.

As you look through these or refer back to them, please see them first as a source of inspiration for specific ideas on how to handle specific problems. Then begin to develop a sense of how to solve all problems with creativity and a can-do attitude.

1. Tomorrow is Friday. For your company that means payday. Time to pass out pay checks to your employees. Time to take home the bacon for you.

Unfortunately, sales have been soft for a full week, or your largest customer is behind in paying you, or you made a substantial error in your check book, or you had to put out a large amount of cash to fix a piece of equipment or . .. any one or two of many things that could happen, and now, you can't make payroll tomorrow.

> **A.** Get on the phone and start calling accounts that owe you money. First call those that are due or past due and attempt to collect. You'll want to get a firm commitment for a check to go out that day. Second, call those that are almost due and ask if they can send the payment now as a favor. If this hasn't created the results you need, call those that are far from due and offer a special discount for early payment, possibly by PayPal or direct to your account.
>
> If some of these accounts are local, you should ask if it would be okay for you to pick up the check. And don't be embarrassed to state your actual need. Don't just say that you can't cover payroll, but give the whole story. "Hi, Bob? I could really use a favor. My receivables have been way off this week, and I'm a bit short to make payroll tomorrow. You have this one item for $535.50 that would just about solve it for me. If you are in a position to help me could I ask you to PayPal the amount or send me a photo of the check front and back." After his agreement: "Bob, I really appreciate this. Let me know when I can return the favor in some way."

    B. Find a customer to take something early. Years ago, it seemed as if our business had a tight cash situation about every other month. One of our customers used to receive a great benefit from this situation. We would call, tell them how much we needed, negotiate a big discount, and deliver the merchandise that day or the next in exchange for a check. In each case this customer probably would have needed the product a month later than we sold it to them. It cost us a pretty penny to get this money, but we needed it, and the customer was more than happy to help out.

    C. Call a supplier to whom you've just mailed a check. See if they have already banked the check. If not, use almost the identical approach as above to persuade them to hold the check for one week.

    D. Start calling anyone you can think of who might be willing to lend you the money for a week or a month, depending on your situation. Let them set the interest rate.

    E. Talk to your employees, starting with managers, to see if they can hold their checks for a few days or take half now and half later. You'll be surprised how often an employee will help in this way and be practically "happy to help." This is another one of those areas where you don't want to ask too often. Happy to help can turn to "this is getting old."

2. One of your primary suppliers is out of product, and can't supply you for six weeks. Sounds far-fetched? I opened a retail bike shop two days before a bicoastal dock strike. Dealers who had been in business for years couldn't get bicycles. I opened on the first of July. I received my first new bike on December 10.

    A. Ask your supplier for ideas. Not just the salesman; go to the production manager, sales manager, marketing manager, vice presidents, and even the president of the supplier. Is there anything they can do to speed the supply?

Is there a substitute available from them? Do they have a foreign subsidiary that makes the same item? Do they have a customer who might be overloaded with that product at this time? Can they recommend a supplier who can solve the problem? You will of course want to assure them that their help in finding you material through another supplier will strengthen your relationship, not cause them to lose a customer.

B. Hit the Web. You may be able to find one or one hundred additional resources within an hour or two of research. Of course, the more options you find, the greater the chance that one will be available at the right time, right price, right terms. Don't correspond with the suppliers found on the Web using e-mail contact information on their "contact us" page.

Or if you do, only do so after trying by phone. The e-mails on these sites are notorious for being dead ends. Even where they are addressed to a real person and not "sales@" or "info@," the recipients commonly have a "not my job" attitude and pass over these unsolicited requests from unknown parties to get to known needs.

If there is no phone number on their Web page, you might have to use one of the few remaining benefits of "Yellow Pages." But of course it will be the Web-based "Yellow Pages." Or if you're rich, call information.

C. Call the appropriate trade association to see if there is a buyer's guide for that industry. If it is not online, have it sent overnight. If there is no buyer's guide, ask the association if they have ideas of who might be able to help—not necessarily just vendor's names, but others who might know who to call.

D. As mentioned before, start calling competitors. Generally, start by calling those that are far enough away not to consider you a threat. You may find someone who has too much. You may just learn of another source or substitute.

E. You can stay in business by dealing with used, reprocessed, or off-spec material (not exactly up to the specifications normally associated with that product).

F. Redirect your attention to a product that can fill the gap. This could either be another product you're already carrying, or it could be a new item.

G. Reduce your overhead to an absolute minimum until the product is available again. Call your landlord and ask for a rent concession. Lay off employees. Cut back your hours of operation. Call suppliers who are due to be paid and ask for an extra thirty days.

Be certain that this experience results in a lesson. If this supplier is the only one carrying this product and it represents an important part of your income, you need to find a way to substantially improve the consistency of supply or change the emphasis of your company.

3. A critical employee quits or can't work.

A. Immediately learn the task yourself, if possible. You'll save money, increase the depth of your company, and give yourself more information about who you should hire.

B. Call a temp service. There are companies offering temporary workers for almost every occupation. You also end up with two additional benefits. If you don't like this person's work, you just call the temp agency and ask them to send someone else. This isn't nearly as emotional as telling someone he's fired.

Furthermore, if the temp turns out to be well qualified and is looking for full-time, permanent work, you can hire him. Some temp agencies have rules regarding some form of compensation for your having hired away their worker, but if the temp is good enough, it's well worth it.

C. Call your supplier salespeople. They may know of someone in the industry who is looking for an opportunity.

D. Think of friends or associates who may be able to fill the gap for a short time. If your spouse is not already working with you, he or she may be able to handle the task until you can find a permanent replacement.

E. Of course you should use the usual hiring approaches such as Indeed, Linkedin, and Monster. However, the above approaches are designed to deal with an emergency where the loss of the employee's talents for even a few days could result in serious problems.

4. You lose your location. You can ensure your building against destruction through fire, flood, or earthquake. You can also purchase business-interruption insurance that is supposed to give you enough staying power to reopen in a new place. What if you don't have that insurance? Or you have a month-to-month rental, and your landlord gives you notice? Maybe you miss a lease payment, and the building's owner holds you to the letter of the lease and kicks you out?

For many businesses, this type of disaster in the early going is all but insurmountable. This is especially so where there has been a large investment in build-outs, signage, or fixtures that can't be easily transferred to a new location. Here are some approaches that might save your bacon.

A. If you have enough capital left for the first and last months' rent on a new location, and believe that you will still have the staying power to save your business, start a dawn-to-dusk search for a new facility. You will probably be far less particular this time. Use two or three real estate agents, but don't count on them alone. Go out and canvass the neighborhood yourself. Some builders and owners don't use an agent, and therefore the property doesn't show up on the listings.

B. If you are really strapped for cash, try to find a building that has been vacant for a long, long time. There will undoubtedly be a reason for this, but you aren't in a very strong position to hold out for prime rental space.

Approach the landlord with a plan that allows you to conserve as much capital as possible while giving up as little as possible. You might be able to move in for free and get one or more months of free rent. If your situation is particularly dire, you might ask for your rent to be a percentage of sales or profit instead of any fixed amount. You might use a combination of fixed plus a percentage.

You could have a fast escalator clause. Maybe you pay nothing the first two months, one hundred dollars the next two, two hundred dollars the next two, and so forth until you are at or slightly above the market rate for this type of location.

C. Can you move the business into your home, garage, a friend's home, garage, or business? Can you sublet a small area in another business? Maybe there is a vendor or customer who has a substantial vested interest in your staying in business. He might be able to provide you with the necessary space until you can afford and find a new location.

D. Consider merging with another similar business. Of course, this means that you'll have all the benefits and detriments of a partnership. However, it might be just the solution.

E. If your cash position is strong, but your chances of finding the right kind of location are weak, consider buying out a competitor.

F. One of the least expensive locations is a mini storage. If all you need is a warehouse, light assembly, or packaging this may be perfect for you. I have known several business owners who have survived in a mini storage for several years.

5. You become temporarily disabled by illness or accident, and are unable to work, or must severely curtail your hours or activity. Once again there is insurance available for this type of situation. Disability insurance is fairly inexpensive and highly recommended by most agents. You may want to carry it during the early phase of your business.

    A. Go back and look at the approaches that were suggested for replacing a critical employee. After all, that is what you are. B, C, and D are very appropriate for this situation.

    B. Check with your suppliers to see if they know of anyone who has retired from the business who might be able to run yours for a while. You might also contact the chamber of commerce and the Small Business Administration for names of individuals who are retired, but who would have the skills necessary to keep you in business until you can get back on your feet.

    C. If you'll be out for only two or three months, would it be possible to simply try to reduce overhead to the lowest possible level, and close up your operation until you can return? Your landlord might be willing to forgo rent for that period or defer it until much later. You can lay off employees, and notify suppliers that you'll be unable to pay them until you return.

6. You are a manufacturer, dentist, restaurateur, or other who depends on equipment for your livelihood. A critical piece of this equipment goes on the blink. The manufacturer tells you the necessary part will not be available for three weeks. How about six weeks? Just for fun, let's say that the three or six weeks pass, and you are now told it will be three or six more, because they sent the wrong part. This is not at all far-fetched.

    A. Your first move should be to work your way up the chain of command of the machine supplier. You will want to let each person in that hierarchy know that you want the necessary part and/or technician at your place of business by the next morning. It is the rare situation indeed that such a part would be so scarce that it would not be able to be found somewhere in the system, such as a reseller of that machine or the parts for it, an end user who has a backup piece of equipment or part, a machine that isn't currently in use, a makeshift part that will work until the right one is ready.

Don't take no for an answer. Insist that your very survival is at stake. Talk to everyone and anyone you can. Somewhere there will be a sympathetic or inventive ear who will find you a solution.

B. If you are a manufacturer, you may have to have your product made for you at a job shop until your machine is back in operation.

C. If you are in the situation of a dentist or similar practitioner, see if any of your friendly competitors has underutilized facilities they would be willing to rent for a time.

D. Again, you may be able to get help by contacting other suppliers. Start with suppliers who are most closely related to that equipment, such as those who provide you with the raw materials you use in that machine.

E. If you get this far without a solution, call the competitive makers of the disabled equipment. They may either help you with a solution in hopes of supplying you with the next machine, or they may be willing to sell you one of theirs with an exchange for the one you now have. This will be especially true if the equipment uses supplies provided by this same vendor.

The six emergency situations cited here are just about the worst things that could happen to you in the early stages of your business. In each case, however, there are numerous solutions available. A can-do attitude mixed with creativity can conquer almost any business problem.

SECTION THREE
Running the Business

1

Why Businesses Succeed

To THE UNINITIATED, business looks pretty easy. Maybe that's why so many try it. Those who have taken the leap know that there is much more to this game than a good idea and some seed money. Henry Ford bankrupted two car companies before his third effort clicked. He is far from alone.

Fortunately, through this book and others like it, you can improve your chances for success. What follows are six very specific ingredients. I believe that if you keep these six elements at the forefront of your thinking, you will succeed. Prior to listing the six ingredients to business success, though, allow me to define the "success" that I'm referring to.

The least that a business can do to be considered successful is survive and pay its owners a living wage. Beyond that, a moderately successful business might pay its owners a wage equal to what they could earn by providing the same services working for someone else. A very successful business will do all the above and repay its investors for their risk at a level commensurate with that risk. The highest level of financial success would include all of these at a very high rate, plus create wealth (value of the enterprise if sold).

Financial success is not the only goal. Many owners would want the business to provide them with a satisfying and challenging career. They might also be looking for certain nonfinancial benefits such as travel, vacation time, or a thirty-hour work week.

In a very small business, the definition of success can become quite wrapped up with the needs of the owner. As mentioned earlier, there should be a separation of these in many instances, but sometimes it is very hard to see the lines of distinction.

Ingredients to Business Success

1. Desire
2. Sales
3. Marketing
4. Luck
5. Accounting
6. Planning

DESIRE

You've got to know what you want and want it *bad!* You must *focus!* You know what you want to accomplish. You knew there would be short-term sacrifices. Maybe you didn't know it would be this hard or take this long. You read section 1, but only believed half of it. You thought you were different. . . better, somehow.

Well, this is the time that separates the champions from the also-rans. Building a successful business is a long race, to be sure, and you are nowhere near the finish line. However, it is your strength and endurance now that will determine if you are even in the race for the second lap. You may not even be as strong as some of the others, but you must want to win more than they do.

Desire includes having a survivor mentality. There must be an underlying feeling in those running the business that failure is not an option. Now this is tricky, because failure *is* a valid option. There is a time and a place where packing it in is the best thing to do. Until that time comes, however, everyone in the organization must believe that folding the tent isn't up for consideration. Such an attitude alone may keep a business right side up for months after others without a survivor mentality have gone broke.

SALES

An associate of mine started a business. Within a year the company had enough sales to break even, but not enough to pay him. At the end of two years his sales were still the same. The overhead was pretty well fixed, so even a small sales increase would have resulted in good profits. From time to time as we discussed his undertaking, I would ask: "If you reached your current sales level in twelve months, why haven't you been able to sell more than that in your second year?"

The answer was simple. He had stopped selling. He was now only servicing his existing accounts. A very small business must maintain a constant sales effort. Selling must be very high on the list of priorities for use of time, energy, and dollars.

MARKETING

You must provide products or services that people need at a price they can afford. If you pass those two hurdles, you must then come up with an effective method of telling your potential customers that you have a great product at a reasonable price. I've experienced times when business has had its greatest growth in product lines from buying out companies who managed to achieve a good product at a right price, but had no idea of how to get the word out.

Finally, you must also establish a method to deliver your product or service to interested customers. Should you sell it direct to the user, or through a series of middlemen? How do you package it? How many distribution centers do you need? Successful businesses understand the options in marketing and use that knowledge as a tool.

LUCK

I list luck fourth. Others I have read would list it first. 1 believe that most luck is made by the hard/smart worker. Nothing irritates me more than hearing someone who hasn't known me long exclaim: "Boy, is he lucky!" This is usually from the lips of someone who has never even walked across a college campus, complains about a forty- hour work week, and spends every evening in front of the tube with a beer in his mitt.

But there is luck (or providence) in the equation. Does the recession hit at a time when you have cash in the bank or when you've just borrowed all the bank will allow? Does the city decide to do roadwork in front of your new restaurant the second week you are open?

One must take the bad with the good. Is it luck when an inventor calls you with a new idea and you end up with a $100 million company? You could say so. However, how did he happen to call you? It could have been your advertising, your reputation, or any number of things you can justifiably feel proud of.

ACCOUNTING

Good accounting can help you in every phase of your business. It's easier to keep your desire intact on even the worst days if you feel that you're in control of your destiny. It's hard to feel in control of any part of your business if you're uncertain about your inventory levels, sales levels, collection effort, cash on hand, production capability, profitability, or even your solvency.

Your sales effort will be vastly improved by supplying those in your sales department with information about how their accounts are doing.

Your marketing will improve if you can accurately determine what you can afford in advertising, promotion, and trade show expense.

Clearly, your planning will be enhanced if you have historical numbers from which to derive your projections.

PLANNING

Planning can move you along your path more quickly. It can help you to miss some of the potholes in the path. It provides you with a mile marker to see how far you've come, and how far there is yet to go. It's a very useful skill and important to the overall success effort.

Conclusion

When I wrote these final words of the first edition in 1993, everyone was complaining about the recession. People were being laid off, businesses were closing. The ozone layer was disappearing, and we were being warned about a new ice age. Maybe that children's fairy tale was right after all. Maybe the sky was falling.

Then again, maybe it wasn't. It certainly wasn't for AC International. Our 1991 sales were 16 percent ahead of 1990's for continuing operations. We recorded a record profit. January of 1992 was running 44 percent better than January of 1991. Our plant was running twenty-four hours per day, seven days per week, and we still couldn't fill the demand. We refused to join the recession.

Did we know something that others didn't? I don't think so. Were we luckier than most businesses? Not at all. Is there a magic bullet that I can pass along? Not one, but several.

1.   Always act as if your business is one month away from going under. Never rest on past success. Constantly scramble, scramble, scramble to retain current business and to find new sales.

2.   Don't pay attention to the doomsayers. Recessions are a part of life. They'll always be with us. Prepare for them, but also prepare for the inevitable growth period that follows.

3.   Do whatever is necessary to get rid of the following emotions: worry, discouragement, bitterness, and despair. Find ways to develop courage, confidence, hope, and a calm spirit.

4.   Learn from others who've blazed these trails before. There is very little new under the sun. Read, listen to tapes, attend seminars, find a mentor or adviser. The more knowledge you have, the more choices you'll have.

5.   Keep this book on top of your desk throughout your business career. You can't possibly absorb all of the information contained herein from just one reading. Use the information that is offered on each subject as a starting point to learn as much as you can about the situations you face.

It's my sincere hope that you'll find as much satisfaction from your career in business as I've found in mine. It's yours for the taking. Good luck and God bless.

Update 2018 – I have spent the last 11 years since the sale of AC International working with over 200 companies as an advisor, coach, consultant. Here are my most recent conclusions, and some of these have articles at https://

1.   Most small businesses are underperforming because of just a single reason. The owner.

2.   The biggest reason why owners are getting in the way of their company's success is a failure to do the hard things.

3.   It is the rare owner who is an expert in every aspect of running a small business. The solution to that is mastermind groups.

4.   I stand by my most important gold nugget: Nothing Happens Until Something Is Sold.

5.   The failure of the owner to lead in the sales effort is the number one hard thing that gets in the way of maximizing the potential of most small businesses.

I am in the process of writing at least five additional books taking deeper dives into some of what is contained in this edition of the book. Much of the future material is provided in a shorter form in the online supplements to this book. Please use these additional materials   at   no   cost   with   my   compliments. **https://WhenFridayIsntPayday.com**

Appendix: Additional Reading

SECTION ONE

Think and Grow Rich by Napoleon Hill

Think and Grow Rich is the basic textbook for salesmanship, for motivation, and for personal achievement. Must read. (Ralston, 1953.)

The Power of Positive Thinking by the Reverend Norman Vincent Peale

No one before or since has done a better job of laying out the techniques for driving negativism out of our lives and learning how to find the positive in everything. (Prentice-Hall, 1952.)

How I Raised Myself from Failure to Success in Selling by Frank Bettger

No other writer I've found deals more fundamentally than does author Frank Bettger with the subject of filling other people's needs. Must read. (Prentice-Hall, 1949.)

The Greatest Salesman in the World by Og Mandino

The basic tenets of professional selling in a succinct, memorable style. (F. Fell, 1968.)

What They Don 't Teach You at the Harvard Business School by Mark McCormack

Street smarts to those of us in the business arena, rather than the highfalutin ideas being handed down by academia. (Ban¬tam, 1984.)

Positioning by Al Ries and Jack Trout

The definitive work on marketing for the late twentieth century. Must read. (McGraw-Hill, 1981.)

Magazines recommended for your monthly reading are: Fortune, Inc., and Boardroom Reports. In addition to these general business publications, you'll want to try to get a subscription to trade journals that are published for the industry you think you may wish to enter. These will give you important insights into suppliers, business methods, the key players, and, most important, industry trends. Check with your librarian or search online.

SECTION TWO

How to Start, Run, and Stay in Business by Gregory F. Kishel and Patricia Gunter Kishel

In chapter 12 Gregory F. Kishel and Patricia Gunter Kishel provide a good overview of business insurance. Chapter 13 offers a checklist to consider if you prefer to go the franchise route. Chapter 14 has lists and lists of places you can go for even more information. (John Wiley and Sons, 1981.)

Tough Times Never Last, but Tough People Do by Robert Schuller

Robert Schuller has written a number of books, but this one is particularly effective at providing the reader with motivation regardless of circumstance. (Thomas Nelson, 1983.)

How to Stop Worrying and Start Living by Dale Carnegie

This classic book should be read by anyone who has ever taken a Turns, chewed his nails, or had problems sleeping because of situations he faced that turned out to be far less of a problem than expected. (Simon & Schuster, 1948.)

The Small Business Administration maintains a program that could be of great help if you run into big problems in the very early going. ACE/SCORE is an organization of retired business people who will come and give you advice on how to handle certain situations. This service is entirely free.

About the Author

Until 2007, when folks asked me what I did for a living and I told them I manufactured bicycle water bottles and Mr. Tuffy tire liners, they looked at me in this quizzical way. I'm not sure whether it was what I manufactured or the fact that I manufactured anything in the USA in these times that causes such an unusual response. Anyway, that's what I did for 28 years.

It wasn't necessarily planned that way. I took an undergraduate degree in psychology at UCLA, intending to help people one or two at a time. Then I took a law degree at the same institution with the goal of helping lots of people. I also love politics. Think of the potential for doing good (or evil) in that field.

Along the way, I fell in love with business—the bicycle business in particular. I tried retail and wholesale, but didn't like being at the mercy of my suppliers. Then I tried sales repping, marketing services, and insuring bikes against theft. But it was manufacturing that was the most satisfying, and that's what paid the bills for twenty-eight years.

Along the way, I wrote a few articles, delivered more than a few talks, and wrote four books for the bicycle industry. After selling AC International in 2007, I did what any ex-manufacturer does, I became a consultant. It was by far the best "job" I've ever had...that is until I started SoCal MasterMinds in 2018. Now I'm helping owners of small businesses in ways I never imagined possible, and it is very fulfilling.

Finally, to round out the picture of your author, I am the proud dad of two grown daughters, who have seven guys and gals for Poppy to play with; and three sons starting their careers. Sharing home duties is my amazing English Professor wife, Toni.

CONTACT THE AUTHOR

If you would like to learn more about joining a SoCal MasterMinds chapter or starting one of your own, please contact me at:

RandyKirk77@gmail.com
Visit our website at https://SoCalMasterMinds.com